**Kartini Centenary
Indonesian Women Then and Now**

Annual Indonesia Lecture Series No. 5

Ailsa Thomson Zainu'ddin
Kadar Lucas
Yulfita Raharjo
Christine Dobbin
Lenore Manderson

Papers given at the annual set of public lectures on Indonesia, organized by the Centre of Southeast Asian Studies, prior to Indonesian Independence Day, August 1979.

Published by
The Centre of Southeast Asian Studies
Monash University
Clayton, Victoria 3168
Australia

© 1980 Centre of Southeast Asian Studies

First printed 1980, reprinted 1995

National Library of Australia

ISBN 0 86746 041 5
ISSN 0729 3623

Contents

Preface	i
Kartini - Her Life, Work and Influence Ailsa Thomson Zainu'ddin	1
Women in a Yogyakarta Kampung Kadar Lucas	23
Women in the Workforce Yulfita Raharjo	29
The Search for Women in Indonesian History Christine Dobbin	42
Rights and Responsibility, Power and Privilege: Women's roles in contemporary Indonesia Lenore Manderson	52
Notes on Contributors	70

Preface

> My friends here say that we shall act wisely if
> we do nothing but sleep for a hundred years.
> When we awaken, Java would be more as we
> would have her.

Kartini to Stella Zeehandelaar, November 6 1899.

Although it is too soon by twenty years to judge whether Java will be more as Kartini would have had her, it seemed appropriate that the Annual Winter Lecture Series, sponsored jointly by the Australia-Indonesia Association of Victoria and the Centre of Southeast Asian Studies, Monash University, should commemorate the centenary of her birth. *Kartini Centenary: Indonesian Women then and Now* has broken new ground in a number of ways. Although the series has been published for half a decade, co-sponsored for about a decade and in existence for almost two decades, this is the first occasion on which the lectures have been planned as a commemoration and comment on the life and work of a single person. In examining the role of Indonesian women then and now, these lectures have picked up the biographical approach begun in the 1976 series as well as examining the other half of Indonesian society until now largely hidden from history.

The opening meeting of the series was chaired by Mrs Lieke Slamet whose grandmother, daughter of the Regent of Kediri, was one of Kartini's pupils, spending most of her school time in Japara and, after Kartini's marriage, following her to the school established the Rembang residence. Mrs Slamet, who has lived in the Netherlands and India as well as in Australia, is a teacher who exemplifies the independence and interdependence of human beings of which Kartini dreamed and the emergence of that self-reliant 'modern girl' whom Kartini so much wished to meet. If we are tempted, with western arrogance, to assume that only 'slumbering Java' needed to awake in regard to the position of women, then we might note that the changes of the past century in Australia were reflected in the fact that Mrs Betty Feith and Dr Margaret Kartomi, who chaired the second and third meetings, are both university graduates teaching at tertiary institutions. In 1879 they would have been denied admission to either of the two universities then established in Australia.

The overwhelming majority of those who attended the first lecture had read Kartini's *Letters* either in the original Dutch or in translation. Her life, work and influence were presented not simply as related to the Javanese society in which she lived, nor as precursor of the Indonesian nation which now reveres her name but as of significance to all who share her concern for letting down 'the bars which have been so foolishly erected between the two sexes' so that 'much good will come of it, especially to the men'.

On the second night of the focus was on Java today as seen by two Javanese women. Kadar Lucas described 'Women in a Javanese Kampung Today' and the network of the relationships which sustains the women who live there. Her paper gives a sensitive portrayal of a community which she knows well and views from both within and from outside. Yulfita Raharjo based her talk, 'Women in the Workforce', on her thesis for Master of Arts in

Demography at the Australian National University, 'Educated Females in the Indonesian Labour Force, 1971: A Socio-Cultural Approach'. The discussion which followed these papers revealed many differing perceptions of women in contemporary Java.

The final lectures, one historical and one sociological, raised wider issues. Christine Dobbin, in 'The Search for Women in Indonesian History', argued convincingly and wittily that, in this search, 'perhaps we can all do better next time'. Lenore Manderson, in 'Right and Responsibility, Power and Privilege: Women's Roles in Contemporary Indonesia', challenged the glib assumption equally glibly made by many governments elsewhere. Her consideration of the comparative roles of women in traditional and contemporary Indonesian society demonstrated 'that most women have attained equality only at a formal and theoretic level'.

The underlying question, 'is Java more as Kartini would have her?' remains unanswered and unanswerable but if, in considering it, women have become more visible than new ground has indeed been broken.

Kartini and her Family

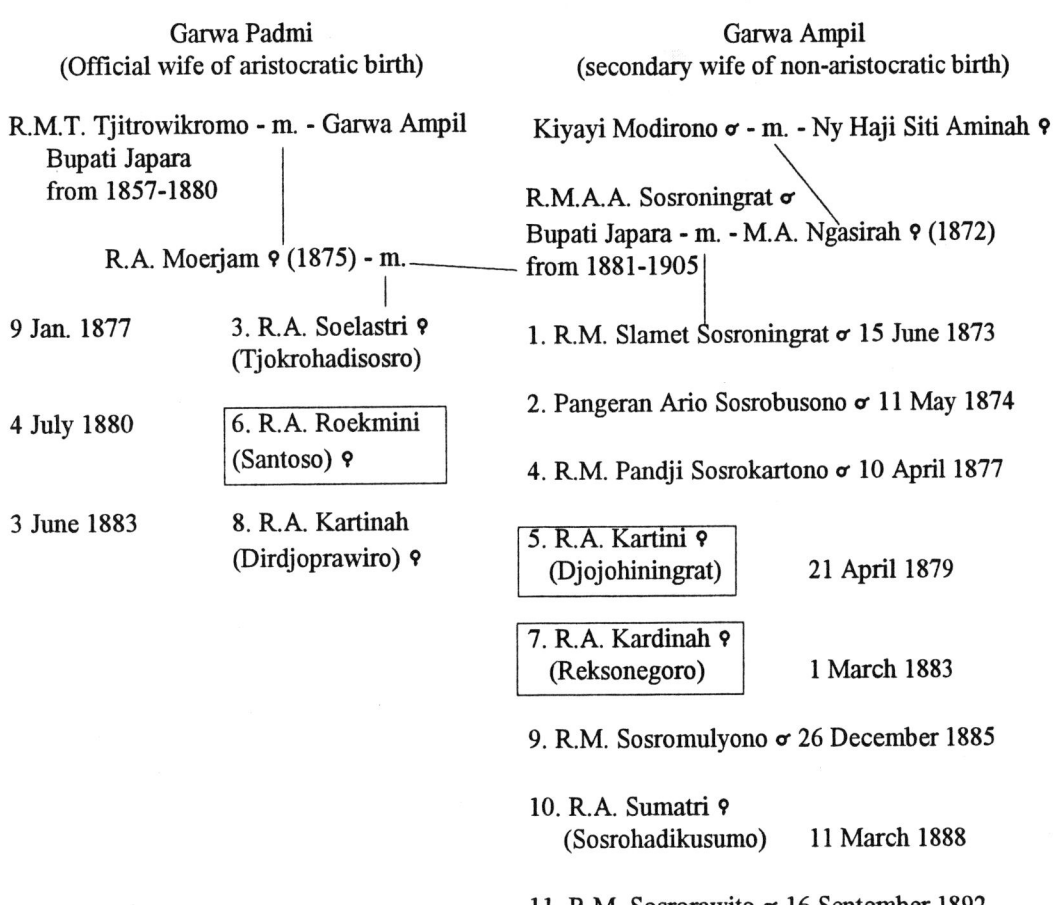

Sources: S.S. Soeroto, *Kartini, Sebuah Biografi* (1977) p. 10. Ibu Kardinah Reksonegoro in *Bijdragen T.L.V. van N.I.* No. 22 1966, p. 286. Heather Sutherland, 'Notes on Java's Regent Families', Part II, *Indonesia*, No. 17, April 1974, Appendix 1.

Kartini - Her Life, Work and Influence

Ailsa G. Thomson Zainu'ddin

1. Childhood (1879-1884)

Kartini was born at Mayong, a small north Javanese town, on 21 April 1879. She was the fifth child and second daughter of Raden Mas Ario Adipati Sosroningrat, who could trace his lineage back to a ruler of Majapahit.[1] A the time of Kartini's birth he was *wedono* of Mayong. Kartini's paternal grandfather was Regent of Demak and several of her uncles were also regents. It was 'a noble and highly placed family—a chain of regents from Java's eastern coast to the middle'.[2] She was the fourth child and first daughter of her mother, Mas Ajeng Ngasirah, who came from a non-aristocratic, wealthy and devout Moslem family. Kartini's parents were married in 1872. In 1875, when it seemed likely that he would soon be appointed as a Regent, her father also married Raden Ajeng Muryam, whose father was Regent of Japara. The *kabupaten*, the Regent's residence, was a large enough estate for two Dutch naval officials new to the place to mistake its driveway for a public road and the house itself for 'a fortress or something of the kind'.[3] Kartini was two when the family moved there, a bright, lively, active little girl whose elder brothers nicknamed her 'Trinil' after the quick-moving little bird of which she reminded them.[4]

With the exception of one visit as far afield as Batavia, returning via Bandung and Yogya, a few brief visits to her family or to Semarang and her last ten months in Rembang, she spent her entire life in this small, remote Javanese coastal town. In 1902 she wrote,

> They that have known Japara, who have seen its soul, can never forget it. They must think of it again and again, whether it is with love or whether it is with hate.[5]

2. Schooling

Kartini's grandfather, Pangeran Ario Tjondronegoro IV, had taken an unusual step when he employed a Dutch tutor for his sons. Kartini's father was thus one of only four regents who, at the turn of the century, could speak Dutch fluently and who had access to the thought and literature of Europe through the Dutch language. He in his turn took the even more unusual step of allowing not only his five sons, but also his six daughters to learn Dutch, not with a tutor in the seclusion of the kabupaten, but by attending the local free primary school established for Dutch and Eurasian children. This privilege was allowed to them because they were the Regent's children.[6] It was the only educational institution in Japara and the girls did

---

[1] *Bijdragen tot de Taal- Land- en Volkenkunde van Nederlandsch- Indie*, Vol. 122, 1966, p.286.
[2] Kartini, *Letters of a Javanese Princess*, transl. from the Dutch by Agnes Louise Symners (1920), ed. And with introduction by Hildred Geertz (Norton Library, N.Y. 1964), (*Letters*), p.42.
[3] *Ibid.*, p.47.
[4] Siti Soemandari Soeroto, *Kartini, Sebuah Biografi* (Gunung Agung, Jakarta 1977), p.32 (Actually the younger children were not allowed to use this nickname as they had to show respect to their elder sister). The other details of Kartini's family and childhood are based on S.S. Soeroto, Chs, 1 & 2, *passim*.
[5] *Letters*, p.196. See map, p.iii.
[6] *Ibid.*, p.32.

not even have to 'cross the road',[7] as Hildred Geertz put it, to reach the school as it was right next door to the kabupaten. Even so, it was a considerable break with tradition. 'Alas! W girls are not allowed by our law [adat] to learn languages: it was a great innovation for us to learn Dutch'.[8] Kartini later told her pen friend, although at the time, of course, she did not realise that her education was at all unusual. One never does until one has something with which to compare it. She was quickly made aware, though, of the differences between her own background and those of the Dutch and Eurasian children at the school. She soon knew that 'it was hard for the teachers to give a native the highest mark, never mind how well it may have been deserved'.[9] She also suffered much ill will, especially from the Eurasian children who formed the majority of her school companions.[10] They did not like to be outstripped, not only by a mere native, but by a girl into the bargain.

Kartini was a lively child, she was never quiet, she was happy at school because she could laugh and move freely and hold her own. Indeed, one of her essays was the best that the inspector of schools had ever seen in the whole inspectorate.[11] Among her school friends was Letsy Detmar, daughter of the school teacher, already planning to be a teacher herself when she was older. It was her question to Kartini, 'What are you going to be when you grow up?' which first made Kartini realise that she herself had no choice in the matter. Her future was subject to 'the ancient iron-bound rule, that girls must marry, must belong to a man, without being asked when, who, or how'.[12]

In the afternoons, after school, Kartini and her sisters, along with their homework also had lessons in embroidery and sewing from a Dutchwoman,[13] learnt to read the Koran from a woman religious teacher who one gathers was not well equipped to parry the many questions raised by the youngsters and also had lessons in Javanese at all levels.[14] As children, they were encouraged to visit the villages and they heard from their father about the sufferings caused by floods and drought, both of which were quite common in that region.[15] They were also provided with plenty of books without any apparent attempt to censor their reading, and they were introduced to various Dutch visitors, often of high rank who came to the kabupaten. This was certainly unusual. At Rembang we were shown the carved screens of the pendopo fretwork on the girls' side and bas-relief on the boys' side and it was explained to us that the fretwork enabled the girls to see the visitors from behind the screen, but it was not needed on the boys' side because they could join the guests).[16]

---

7   *Ibid.*, (Introduction), p.11.
8   *Ibid.*, p.55.
9   *Ibid.*, p.58.
10 Interview with Ibu Kardinah Reksonegoro, Salatiga, 11 March 1970. 'The Indos did not want to have anything to do with the Indonesians. They were worse than the Dutch'.
11 S.S. Soeroto, *op. cit.*, pp.44.
12 *Letters*, p.71; S.S. Soeroto, *op. cit.*, p.45.
13 Mrs Ovink-Soer, wife of the Assistant resident (see *Letters*, p.46 and ftn. 28).
14 S.S. Soeroto, *op. cit.*, pp.34-5, cf, *Letters*, p.44 and p.182.
15 Eg, *Letters*, pp.51-5, p.126.
16 This suggests that Rembang was more traditional than Japara where the girls were permitted to meet European guests, cf. *Letters*, pp.46-48.

After six years of schooling, when Kartini was twelve, she was expected to retire into seclusion regarded as appropriate for an adolescent aristocratic Javanese girl prior to the marriage, which would be arranged by her parents. The end of primary school meant the end of childhood freedom. She begged and pleaded to be allowed to continue her education at Semarang, the nearest high school, where her brothers were sent but that would have meant living away from home in her adolescent years and it was seen as too great a break with tradition.[17] Later Kartini, in reflecting on the effects of her schooling, commented that:

> I had rather have my whole life one of strife and sorrow than be without the knowledge which I owe to my European education ... they say that it was a mistake for my father to give me the little education which I have had. No! No! Not on my dearest father lies the blame. No, and again no! Father could not foresee that the same bringing up which he gave to all of his children would have had such an effect upon one of them.[18]

Apart from the work that she did later under the guidance of Annie Glaser (August 1901 to August 1902)[19] she had no other formal schooling.

3. Pingitan - The Adolescent Years (1892-96-98)

Kartini was to look back on the first four years of her seclusion, from 1892 to 1896 as sheer hell, 'locked up and cut off from all communications with the outside world'.[20] Hers was a stormy adolescence. She fought bitterly with her oldest brother, refusing to bow to the authority he exercised by virtue of being a boy and older than she and her opposition was even more bitter because she recognised the extent to which this male egoism had been developed and encouraged by the women of the house-hold.[21] She clashed with her older sister who said reprovingly, 'Go your own way; as for me, I am a Javanese', whenever Kartini queried or resisted the pressures of Javanese etiquette.[22] She 'watched her younger sisters with hungry longing' as they set forth for school each morning.[23] She longed passionately 'to be free, to be able to stand alone, to study, not to be subject to anyone, and above all, *never, never* to be obliged to marry'.[24]

Although she suffered deeply during this time, even then she was in many ways less cut off from the outside world than other girls of her class at that time. The main difference was that she knew of the existence of that outside world and longed to participate in its activities. She read voraciously.[25] She read Mrs Goekoop's *Hilda van Suylenburg* 'through in one sitting. I locked myself in our room and forgot everything; I could not lay it down, it held me so'. In another letter she wrote: '... I have read three times. I could never grow tired of it. What

---

17 *Letters*, p.72.
18 *Ibid.*, p.41.
19 S.S. Soeroto, *op. cit.*, p.229, p.263. See also *Letters* (Introduction) p.17 and pp.129, 167, 195-6.
20 *Letters*, pp.32-3.
21 *Ibid.*, pp.75-6. 'She would never give in to her brother except when she was convinced he was right'.
22 *Ibid.*, p.74. After the elder sister had married she seems to have become more sympathetic to Kartini's views (cf. *Letters*, p.140). One wonders why.
23 *Ibid.*, p.73.
24 *Ibid.*, pp.33-4.
25 *Ibid.*, pp.77-8.

would I not give to be able to live in Hilda's environment ... I shall never rest till H. Van S appears in my own language to do good as well as harm to our Indian world'.[26] The book was the story of a woman who tried to support herself alone in the face of social criticism. Kartini knew that she had the support of Kartono, her third brother, two years her senior, though he never told her so directly. 'She knew that he was only silent because he did not want to make her more rebellious. The books which he placed in her hands showed her that'.[27]

She was also permitted to spend an hour a day, provided that she went there by carriage, at the home of the Assistant-Resident, having sewing lessons with his wife, Mrs Ovink-Soer, herself a cultivated woman with feminist sympathies. In modern terminology she provided a role-model for Kartini and when she and her husband moved to Jombang, Kartini wrote at the end of 1899:

> O little mother ... I wish that you were back with us. Your daughters miss you so much ... I miss the intimate talks with you, when I used to tell my dear little mother all the rebellious thoughts that came into my head and laid bare the feelings of my restless heart.

Mrs Ovik-Soer in her recollections of Kartini, remembered her saying in 1895:

> Ah, Ibu, I want to live a hundred years. This life is so short. There is so much work waiting to be done ... and now I am not yet able to start.[28]

By the time Kartini was sixteen, life began to improve a little. Her elder sister married and moved to her new home. The eldest brother was posted elsewhere, much to Kartini's rather guilty relief.[29] Her favourite brother, Kartono, also left for the Netherlands in 1896[30] and Kartini was then the oldest child at the kabupaten. By this time her two younger sisters, Roekmini and Kardinah, had joined her in seclusion and she, as the eldest of this very close-knit trio, introduced a more informal relationship between them, dropping some of the aspects

---

26 *Ibid.*, p.64, 35.
27 *Ibid.*, p.75. Ibu Kardinah (11.3.1970) spoke of the closeness between Kartini and Kartono who later became a faith healer. He had a great influence on Kartini.
28 *Letters*, pp.48-9; S.S. Soeroto, *op. cit.*, p.90. Their handicraft was of sufficiently high standard for the three sisters to submit eleven separate items to the National Exposition of Women's Work, held in the Netherlands in 1898. These include landscapes, embroidery of tulips and birds on satin, paintings on satin, on glass, on shells and on imitation leather, carved bamboo as well as tie-dying and the exhibit (No. 251) of the whole process of batik work. Amsterdam, *Nationale Tentoonstelling van Vrouwenarbeid, Catalogue and Reports* (available in microfiche in the Gerritsen Collection, State Library of Victoria, items 72, 72.1 and 73). The list of items submitted by the three sisters is on p.349 (no.72, Card 4) and the batik exhibit is also cited in Rouffaer, G.P. and Juynbool, Dr H.H. *De Batikkunst ...* (Batik in NEI and its History), Mevr C. Goekoop- De Jong van Beek en Donk, the author of *Hilda van Suylenberg*. (Various items in the Gerritsen collection refer to this work and Item 1438 contains the text of the 2nd ed., Leiden, 1898). See also *Letters*, p.150.
29 *Letters*, p.79.
30 S.S. Soerto, *op. cit.*, p.90. Clearly her desire to join the brother to whom she felt so close must have been one element in Kartini's desire to study in the Netherlands. He continued living there for thirty years. See also *ibid.*, pp.156-63 and *Letters*, p.130.

of Javanese etiquette which she found so 'silly and terrible'.[31] They called themselves the *Three Sisters* or *Three-fold Clover Leaf* and they made plans for the future in the hope that together they might be given greater freedom than any one of them could hope for on her own. In that same year—1896—their father allowed them to accept an invitation to the dedication of a new church at Kedung Panjalin[32] and Kartini caught her first glimpse of the world outside the kabupaten since her school-days. Two years later they were permitted to accept an invitation Semarang to attend the Governor General's reception which was held to celebrate the coronation of Queen Wilhelmena. Kartini's parents, by supporting the girls to this extent, were much more progressive than other regents were prepared to be. Within Javanese aristocratic circles there was much criticism of this overt break with tradition and it could hardly have been more public than at this particular celebration.[33]

4. Struggle for Independence and the Right to Work (1899-1903)

The fourth period of Kartini's life, her struggle for autonomy and freedom, for a career and permission to prepare for and pursue it, covers the four years in which all but the last ten of her letters were written. It began in 1899, the year in which Stella Zeehanelaar answered Kartini's request for a pen friend in a Dutch feminist magazine.[34] What Kartini wanted was the right to an independent life of her own. In 1899 she declared to Stella that:

> I would do the humblest work, thankfully and joyfully, if by it I could be independent ... It is only work for pleasure which would not be a disgrace to my noble and highly placed family ... Why did God give us talents and not the opportunity to make use of them?[35]

In the following year, J.H. Abendanon was appointed as Minister for Instruction, Religion and Labour. In August of that year he and his wife visited Japara and one reason was to meet the three girls. In a letter to Mrs Abendanon-Mandri written shortly after the visit Kartini said:

> Later, when we have flown from the warm parental nest and are in the midst of ordinary human life, where no faithful parent's arm is thrown protectively around

---

31 *Letters*, p.38.
32 *Ibid.*, p.202. This seems to have been about 10km from Japara.
33 *Loc. cit.* It is easy to overlook the extent to which Kartini's parents were themselves progressive for the time and prepared to support their daughters and their support and sympathy are perfectly clear to Kartini even when these fail to satisfy her needs for greater autonomy.
34 S.S. Soeroto, *op. cit.*, pp.126-7. Stella, five years Kartini's senior, answered her letter in *De Hollandsche Lelie* (The Dutch Lily). Stella's father had died when she was young. She had finished her secondary education as ward of an uncle before working in the Postal Department in Amsterdam. She was a member of the Social Democratic Worker's Party. Although she later married, she did not at the time of their correspondence, have a very high regard for men. She served as Kartini's *alter ego* and yet, fatherless herself, she was perhaps ill-equipped to appreciate fully the close bond between father and daughter and the resulting ambivalence of Kartini, torn between her duty to and love for her father and her own need for autonomy. Stella fully understood and supported the latter, but perhaps not the former. See *Letters*, p.127, and S.S. Soeroto, *op. cit.*, pp.126-8.
35 *Letters*, p.42.

us ... then for the first time, you will see what we are ... Still a whole life-time lies before us; let us see what can be made of it.[36]

What Kartini wanted was for the three girls to continue their education, preferably in the Netherlands, but, failing that, in Batavia and then to establish a secondary vocational boarding school for aristocratic girls so that they would have an alternative to forced arranged marriages. Mr Abendanon supported her cause and a subsidy was granted for the three sisters to study in Batavia at the Girls High School (HBS) there. At the same time, Mr Abendanon sent a circular to other regents inquiring what they thought about the idea and the replies to this circular, to Kartini's great disappointment, indicated that there was insufficient support among other regents for the school which Kartini wished to see established. The plans were further upset by the marriage of the youngest of the trio, Karinah, to her cousin on 24 January 1902.[37] While the other two were recovering from the shock of this separation, an even more powerful advocate appeared. Van Kol, Social Democratic Labour Party member of the Netherlands Parliament, through Stella, had arranged to meet them on his tour of the Netherlands Indies and on his return he persuaded the home government to award the two remaining sisters scholarships to study in the Netherlands.[38] Kartini's often expressed dream of studying in Europe seemed on the verge of fulfilment.

As soon as Mr Abendanon heard of this scholarship, he and his wife went straight to Japara and on 24 January 1903, he persuaded Kartini that such a move would alienate them from the people they wished to teach. This was exactly a year from the marriage of Karinah. Abendanon chose as the setting for the attempt to persuade Kartini, the seashore Klein Scheveling, of which she was particularly fond and his argument was based on serving the cause. He also argued that she did not really need any further education or certification before opening a school for girls. It is doubtful whether either Abendanon or Van Kol fully appreciated Kartini's educational plans. Like Kartini's father, Abendanon seems to have seen the proposed school as simply 'work for pleasure', a hobby rather than a calling or a vocation. The girls were still firmly imprisoned in the 'warm parental nest' and this time, seemingly, of their own choice. Siti Soemandari Soeroto, in her biography of Kartini, argues convincingly that this was a tragic mistake, a denial of herself and her principles from which Kartini never recovered.[39]

She had written earlier to Mrs Abendanon-Mandri:

> You have certainly heard many times of the enviable calmness with which the Javanese meets the most frightful blows of destiny. It is *takdir*—foreordained, they say and are submissive ... Against *takdir* nothing in the world can prevail ... That is why our people would not eat themselves forever against that which had

---

36 *Ibid.*, p.68.
37 *Ibid.*, p.107, 151-61. Kartini's letter to Mrs Abendanon-Mandri (29 November 1901), esp. P.134, seems also to refer to Kardinah's approaching wedding. See also p.141, 'when the great blow fell, we felt nothing'.
38 *Ibid.*, p.149, 165-9, 185. She wrote to Stella, regarding the journalist who accompanied Van Kol, 'I only hope that making our ideas public will do good and not harm', a premonition perhaps.
39 S.S. Soeroto, *op. cit.*, pp.189-90.

actually happened. Brought face to face with a fact, they are face to face with *takdir* and are submissive. God give us strength.[40]

So Kartini and Roekmini refused the scholarship to the Netherlands. They tried without success, to have it passed on to Agus Salim, a young Minangkabau of whom people were to hear a lot more later.[41] They applied again for financial assistance to study in Batavia, this time for two rather than three of them. They could not just go back and take the other subsidy that was granted, because that was for three and one knows all about official channels and bureaucracy. They had to start all over again with new application because now there were only the two of them. Until they heard from the government there was nothing they could do to further their long-term plans. In June they began a small school in the Kabupaten for children eight to ten years.[42] In the second week of July Kartini received a further shock. The Bupati of Rembang, a friend of her father over the past two years, had six children. His young *garwa padmi* (official wife) had recently died. He approached Kartini's father with a proposal of marriage to Kartini. She wag given three days in which to decide—not quite an arranged marriage. She still had no guarantee that the plan to study in Batavia would fare any better than the plan to study in the Netherlands. She had been told so often that, as a married woman, she might hope for more freedom of action than she could ever hope to attain as a single woman. Her father had always responded to her requests to write for publication that she should write 'later'.

> I knew what the 'later' meant ... when I should have become harmless, by having the R. Ajeng changed to R. Ayu.

And she had written in a moment of bitterness to Mrs Abendanon-Mandri:

> Much, yes everything, can be taken away from me, but not my pen—that will always be mine.[43]

So at the end of the three days she had to decide. She was twenty four and still unmarried. She had been under continuous pressure to consider marriage since she was sixteen. She had resited this pressure for a long time but of course the pressure did not stop. Her father's illness must also have influenced her. She had at one stage considered staying with her father while the two younger girls went to Europe. An unmarried woman of noble birth, should her father die, would be at the mercy of her elder brother, 'her future protector, whenever she should have the misfortune to lose her parents'. He may well have chosen to settle old scores to exercising his right to 'marry her off'. Her only protection against this would be if he wished to marry her to someone of lower status. According to Javanese opinion, the Regent of Rambang was eminently eligible and she may have hoped for understanding and support

---

40 *Letters*, pp.204-5.
41 This letter is omitted from the English translation, although mentioned in the preface (p.16) by Hildred Geertz.
42 *Letters*, pp.222-3.
43 *Ibid.*, pp.138, 200.

for her work.[44] Her acceptance of the proposal was conditional upon a promise from her future husband, considerably older than she was, to agree with her ideas and allow her to open a school for girls at Rembang similar to that at Japara. He agreed, she accepted.

Meanwhile, on 7 July the Governor General had signed the authorization for a subsidy for Kartini and Roekmini to study in Batavia. This approval was making its leisurely way through the bureaucratic system when the proposal of marriage came. It finally reached Kartini at Japara on 24 July and once again she had to refuse the opportunity she had so desperately wanted to accept. The offer had come too late.[45] In terms of her own personal struggle for autonomy she was facing again the situation of which she had written in August 1900 in one of her earliest letters to Mrs Abendanon-Mandri. Then she was talking about her seclusion after her school years. She wrote of the three sisters:

> ... And now that their eyes have grown accustomed to the light, now that they have learned to love the sun and everything that is in the brilliant world, they are about to have the blinders pressed back against their eyes and to be plunged into the darkness from which they had come and in which each and everyone of their grandmothers back through the ages had lived.[46]

5. Marriage (1903-4)

On 8 November 1903, in a ceremony kept simple at the bride's request,[47] Kartini became official wife (*garwa padmi*) of the Bupati of Rembang and moved to her new home at the kapubaten there. In the few letters she wrote announcing the coming marriage she referred to her husband as a widower with six children, We do not know at what stage Kartini herself discovered that her husband also had three secondary wives (*garwa ampil*) at the kabupaten. She did not try to correct the impression she had given in any extant letters to European friends. Certainly her father, her beloved father whom she respected and loved and whom she so resembled in character, must have known this as he and Kartini's future husband had first met and become good friends in 1901. Kartini had told Stella that:

> Father knows that I wish to become at any price, free, independent and unshackled, and that I could never be happy in a married life as marriages are now, and have always been.

In the same month she had written to Stella:

> If father should marry me off in this manner then I should find a way out at the beginning, one way or another. But then father would never do that.[48]

---

44 *Ibid.*, pp.128; 76 (I am indebted to Betty Feith for drawing this point to my attention); p.132. She was also concerned about malicious gossip (*Letters*, pp.199, 241) arising from her defiance of convention.
45 S.S. Soeroto, *op. cit.*, pp.346-7.
46 *Letters*, p.69.
47 *Ibid.*, p.228.
48 *Ibid.*, pp.92, 82.

Presumably he believed that he had at least given her some degree of choice. She could still have said 'no' just as she could have rejected the arguments of Abendanon and said 'yes' to the scholarship. This too was something she had already considered. There was a lot of time for considering during her years of seclusion.

> There is nothing new under the sun; [she wrote to Mrs Abendanon-Mandri in 1901] ... long ago in old times there were rebellious daughters too. It has always been preached to us that it was our duty to belong blindly to our parents. At the same time it had happened that when a young woman, submissive to their decree, was married and afterwards unhappy, they would make sport of her and say: 'Foolish one, why then did you marry? When you were married, you were willing ... you must not complain now'.[49]

Both her biographer, Siti Soemandari Soeroto and her husband's granddaughter, Professor Dr Haryati Soebadio, writing in the *Indonesian Quarterly*, agree that 'Kartini's happy sounding letters with regard to her marriage and the man she married' should not be taken at face value.[50]

Neither her father nor her husband had really understood how deeply or passionately she resented the notion of polygamy and its implication for women. How could they be expected to understand? By the standards of the time any person who had only two wives, one official and one secondary—as her father did—and who treated all his children as equals—as her father also did—was unusual. Kartini mentioned a regent's daughter in Sunda with fifty-three mothers and eighty-nine siblings. Kartini's husband had three secondary wives and the six children who formed the nucleus of her school at Rembang were their children.[51] The official wife, whom Kartini replaced, had died without issue. Professor Dr Haryati Soebadio had said:

> To a man of his upbringing and position no woman, even a future padmi, should worry about his private life. That was his own business. From what my mother told me about her father, he certainly seemed to have been a man who knew and always did what he wanted. He was modern enough and always did what he wanted. He was modern enough in many ways, but in his relationship to women he fully belonged to his time.[52]

We must also remember that prior to the publication of her letters in 1911, Kartini's views on polygamy had been expressed privately, not publicly. In the last extant letter to Stella she wrote:

> The public must not know what we are really fighting—the name of the enemy against which we take the field must never, never be cried aloud—it is polygamy.

---

49 *Ibid.*, p.133.
50 *Op. cit.*, vol. 6, no.2, 1978, p.96.
51 *Letters*, p.137. We should also remember that her husband with only three secondary wives was within the limits approved by Islam.
52 *Indonesian Quarterly*, vol. 6, No. 2, 1978, p.99.

If that word were heard no man would trust his child to us. I have struggled against this, for it is as though we began our work with a lie.[53]

Although she wrote of her plans for the school after the birth of her baby and even said:

Now we shall have something á la *Hilda van Suylenburg*—a mother who with suckling baby goes to work.

Her last letters look backward rather than forward.

I live in the past, that sweet and that bitter past when I was so eager for suffering and where your love is interwoven always like a garland of light. I suffered and rejoiced.[54]

she wrote to Mrs Abendanon-Mandri.

For many readers, the poignant paragraph in the Letters is the one where she writes:

If the child that I carry under my heart is a girl, what shall I wish for her? I shall wish that she may live a rich full life and that she may complete the work that her mother has begun. She shall never be compelled to do anything abhorrent to her deepest feelings. What she does must be of her own free will. She shall have a mother who will watch over the welfare of her innermost being, and a father who will never force her into anything. It will make no difference to him if his daughter remains unmarried her whole life long; what will count with him will be that she shall always keep her esteem and affection for us.[55]

The child was a boy and four days after his birth his mother died. She was only 25.

*****

Kartini's Work and Influence
Having divided Kartini's life into five parts like the fingers of one hand, the principles of Pancasila, the pillars of Islam and the *pendawa*, I originally planned to do this with her work and influence.

We could consider, for example, her role as the product of a *Ethical Policy* at its best, a product of the policy, a participant, a proponent and also a victim of it. Kartini was Abendanon's protege. He supported her proposal for girls' schools, or at least his own version of this, and carried it through after her death, but he also made a special trip to Japara to persuade her to give up her cherished scholarship for the sake of the cause as he saw it. Siti Soemandari Soeroto, in her biography of Kartini, points out that a people whose education had been neglected for so long could hardly be in any sudden or great danger from such

---

53 *Letters*, p.221.
54 *Ibid.*, pp.241, 243.
55 *Ibid.*, p.240. (NB the date given in the original Dutch is '8th' and not '28th').

neglect should two young girls delay opening a school for a few years longer while they studied to become teachers.[56] Abendanon betrays a certain unconscious condescension when he assures Kartini that she needs no further preparation to teach girls or to become a writer.

Siti Soemandari Soeroto also shows that Abendanon's special visit and strong opposition occurred after he had heard about the connection between Kartini and Van Kol. Whether this revealed a resentment on the part of a Netherlands Indies Government official of interference from a Netherlands politician, or whether it was perhaps more political than that, or more personal, we do not know. Certainly Stella believed that 'Kartini was sacrificed for the interests of the Netherlands Indies Government' as she wrote to Mrs Van Kol.[57] Professor Dr Haryati Soebadio speculates that possibly Kartini's penfriends with their socialist and feminist leanings may have endangered her father's position as *bupati* so that his desire to see her married might also have been for his own sake and for that of the family, a further pressure to give up her own selfish desires for the good of those she loved.[58]

In the second place, we might examine her role as a *Pioneer of National Independence*, a role formally recognised in 1964 when her sister, Ibu Kardinah Reksonegoro, accepted the award on her behalf sixty years after her death.[59] In 1911 the publication of Kartini's letters was celebrated by the Indies Union of students studying in the Netherlands. Raden Mas Notosoeroto spoke on 'The Ideals of Kartini as a Guide to the Indies Union', urging its members to develop her ideas of a healthy nationalism which is prepared to admit its faults and to take elements which are good from other people.[60] Cora Vreede-de Stuers, in a recent article in *Archipel*, suggested that Kartini as pioneer and forerunner of independence may perhaps be given some credit for the wording of the Youth Pledge of 1928 which was taken by 'We the young men and women of Indonesia'.[61] (One might compare it with the opening line of *Advance Australia Fair!*). And in that connection it is perhaps also worth noting that the author of *Indonesia Rays*, the national anthem, also wrote *Ibu Kita Kartini*[62] the national song sung on Kartini Day, 21 April.

It can be argued that Kartini herself had no coherent theory of nationalism and so was not consciously a pioneer. It can also be argued that she was extremely deferential to her Dutch

---

56 p.289.
57 qu. *Ibid.*, p.333.
58 *Op. cit.* It is possible also that Kartono, who by 1925 was list in Netherlands official reports as a PNI tember (Rapport betreff de neutraliseering en Bestrijding van Revolutionnaire Propaganda onder de inheemsche Bevolking in het bijzonder van Java en Madoe No. 29) may have been regarded as having doubtful associations. Both her beloved brother and her 'twin-soul' penfriend may thus have contributed to the ultimate tragedy.
59 S.S. Soeroto, *op. cit.*, p.437 gives us the text of the award.
60 *Ibid.*, pp.401-4.
61 *Archipel 13* Numero Special: Regards sur les Indonesiennes, p. 116. (SECMI 1977). Instead of having any recognition of the common bonds between young men and women the opening words of *Advance Australia Fair* are 'Australia's *sons* let us rejoice ...'
62 Our Mother Kartini. Sukarno is said to have changed the original 'Raden Ajeng Kartini', which emphasised the status as a single woman, which she sought to preserve, to the symbolic 'Mother of us all', the inclusive 'we' (kita). In his book on women, *Sarinah*, he mentions Kartini only twice and was clearly incapable of grasping the central content of her message. He contributed heavily to the mythologising of Kartini, elevating her to the pedestal of 'national heroine'.

friends and saw a continuing association in which they led the way.[63] In this connection it should be remembered that she was writing to friends, most of them considerably older than she was, and that her letters were edited by Abendanon. Against this one could point to the interest in Agus Salim and her desire to be in touch with other educated young men, such as Abdul Muis.[64] She showed interest also in the Sundanese bupati's daughters whom she met on-her visit to Bandung and may even have corresponded with them. She became a symbol of nationalism and the ideal of Young Java could scarcely have been fulfilled without breaking down the barriers between the sexes.

When Sukarno was on trial in 1930 he referred in his defence to 'the promise of a brightly beckoning future'[65] which echoed the conclusion of Hatta's defence of himself in the Netherlands in 1928. 'The red radiance of the future already begins to dawn in the present. We greet it as the dawn of a new day'.[66] Kartini, in 1901, had written to Mrs Abendanon:

> Through darkness and mist we see the splendid light break, which beckons us with friendly hands. It is the light of our ideal! We know now that we shall never be able to cease from striving; it has grown to be part of our being—of our very existence.[67]

In the third place we could examine her ideas on the role and function of Education as a means of bridging the gulf which separates nation from nation, class from class and sex from sex. Abendanon included, with the letters he published, her paper 'Educate the Javanese'.[68] It was dropped from the English Letters, perhaps because it did not fit with the translator's preoccupations, but has been translated into English by Jean Taylor. Kartini herself was the second generation of her family to participate in Western education. Both her uncle and her father had prepared memoranda which advocated the extension of Dutch language education and its use as the medium of administration. Her brother Kartono had spoken at the 25th Congress of Dutch Language and Literature in Gent in 1899 (he was 22 at the time) advocating the same thing.[69] Kartini's memorandum must have been written in a very short

---

63 *Letters*, pp. 174; 99, 162; 180; 188.
64 *Ibid.*, pp. 119-20.
65 Feith H. and Castles, L. (eds.), *Indonesian Political Thinking, 1945-1964*, (Cornell U.P., 1970), p. 32.
66 Hatta, Moh., *Portrait of a Patriot, Selected Writings* (ed. Deliar Noer Mouton, 1972), p. 293.
67 *Letters*, p.131. I would not wish to overstate this point. Charles Coppel rightly pointed out in discussion that this was part of the whole spirit of the age—bringing light to the heathen, all the early publications of nationalist journals (such as *Pelita*), Abendanon's choice of title for the letters—and suggested that this makes it inadequate to refer back to Kartini. Nevertheless, she was a pioneer of much nationalist thought with an unquenchable belief in the ultimate triumph of the new age. This was the first time that anyone had written in this way, that private letters had been published. The point about the oath is imply that, because with the blessing and at the instigation of the Dutch, this earliest publication was so widespread and because it was by a woman, the nationalist movement could not just ignore one half of the population as was done in Australia, for example. As Professor K.E. Fitzpatrick has said, 'There is no limited liability in the business of human freedom'. Kartini was the sort of person who criticised according to one standard, whatever she saw—Javanese tradition, the way the Dutch spoke in comparison with the way they acted, liberation between the sexes. There is a whole spectrum from which can be drawn the one thread which could lead toward nationalism.
68 *Indonesia*, No. 17, April 1973, pp.83-98.
69 *Neerlandia*, October 1899 (Photocopy in my possession with annotations by the late Amin Singgih).

time straight after her voluntary renunciation of her own educational aspirations. It draws together many of the educational points raised in her letters and many of the issues which would have been discussed in the family. She had been asked to do this by a highly placed official from the Ministry of the Colonies at a time when, as Jean Taylor reminds us, 'no woman's opinion had ever been sought by the colonial government'[70] or for that matter by many other governments of that time or later, colonial or not.

In the fourth place, we could look at other aspects of her work as an *Intellectual and a Writer*. Her father discouraged her from writing for publication because it attracted undesirable notoriety. 'It is good for you to be versed in the Dutch language', says Father, 'but you must not make that an excuse for telling your inmost thoughts'. Yet he had submitted an article written by Kartini to *Bijdragen tot de Taal-, Land- en Volkenkunde van Nederlandsch-Indie*, and this was published in 1899.[71] She corresponded both with the scholar Dr Adriani, a missionary and linguist who worked among the Pamona on Lake Poso in Central Sulawesi, and with Professor and Mrs Anton from Jena. This scholarly aspect of Kartini did not particularly interest her translator.

In the fifth place, we could see her as a *Pioneer of Womanhood*.[72] She put great stress on the role of motherhood both actual and spiritual[73] while at the same time she struggled for the right to be independent and autonomous. Takdir Alisjahbana has claimed that 'to this very day there has never been a woman's group in Indonesia who has made demands more radical than Kartini's'.[74] It is not an aggressive feminism, but simply one which perceives and presents the fundamental issues and refuses to accept the notion of a double standard.

'I should so love to have children' she writes,

> ... but above all things I should never follow the unhappy custom of putting boys before girls... I should teach my children, boys and girls, to regard one another as equal human beings and give them always the same education; of course following the natural disposition of each.
>
> I should not allow my girl, although I wished to make a new woman of her, to study as though she had no other desire in life; nor would I cut her off in anything so that her brother could have more. Never!
>
> And then I should let down the bars which have been so foolishly erected between the two sexes. I am convinced that when this is done much good will come of it, especially to the men.

---

70 Jean Taylor, *op. cit.*, Introduction, p. 85.
71 *Letters*, p. 138; *Bijdragen TLV van NI*, Vol. 6, VI, 1899, pp. 698-700, sent in by the Regent of Japara. Kartini was sixteen when she wrote the article on the Arabs of Java, showing here the same lively interest in other customs and other ways of life which again seems to suggest a sensitivity to unity in diversity. (cf. *Letters*, p. 207, also pp. 172-3, re Chinese girls).
72 Although I put this last, in my own interpretation I see it as central to her whole life and thought.
73 *Letters*, p. 97 and esp. pp. 194-5.
74 Alisjahbana, T. *Indonesia: Social and Cultural Revolution* (OUP, 1966), p. 107.

She also wrote,

> We wish to form an alliance with our enlightened progressive men, to seek their friendship and after that their cooperation with us. We are not giving battle to men but to old moss-grown edicts and conventions...[75]

I do not want to pursue these themes any further at the present though they could well be expanded.

Whatever aspect of Kartini's life, work and influence we pursue we come back to the letters. It is through Kartini's letters that we know her. I first discovered them myself when I was in that post-marital post-natal seclusion, which is perhaps the nearest thing in Australian society to the Javanese aristocratic pre-marital *pingitan*. I came upon a 1921 English edition published by Duckworth and Co., London.[76] It was in the State Library of Victoria in the time when it still had a lending section—and that was before the era of photocopying. I was so fascinated by the *Letters*, not then available in Melbourne, that I typed out 45 pages of foolscap single spacing before I could bear to return the book.

Because it is through her letters that we know her we need to consider what we actually know about the letters. They were published in 1911, after having been collected and edited by J.H. Abendanon, in their original Dutch under the title *Door Duisternis Tot Licht* (Through Darkness to Light, Thoughts of R. Adj. Kartini).[77]

Abendanon had a double purpose in publishing the letters. In the first place they provided an excellent example of the effects of Western education. As former Minister of Education, Religion and Industry for the natives of the Netherlands Indies, he saw these letters as a vindication of the policy which had been regarded as 'too progressive' and had led to his recall in 1904. This young Javanese girl had had only six years of formal schooling and had lived her whole life in a small isolated Javanese town yet through her knowledge and command of the Dutch language she had gained access to the culture of the West.

His second reason was that he wanted to use the royalties from the letters to carry on the work of educating Javanese girls, continuing the plan which Kartini had advocated. Mrs Soemandari Soeroto argues that he should perhaps also have felt some degree of responsibility for the contribution he made to her relinquishment of the plan to go to Europe,[78] followed so closely by her marriage and subsequent death. In any case, he found that he had a best seller and by 1912 the book had reached its third edition. In 1920 an English translation was published in America and in 1922 the first Indonesian language

---

75 *Letters*, pp. 83; 66, cf. S. S. Soeroto, *op. cit.*, p. 338.
76 A show of hands indicated that the majority of those in the audience had read them, several more than once, some in bot the original and either the English or the Indonesian translation. The Duckworth edn. was not listed in the *Archipel* bibliography. See fn. 79.
77 I sometimes find myself drawing a comparison between this ambiguous title and that of an even larger three-volume work *Vision and Realisation*, the centenary history of the Victorian Education Department (1972). There is no resemblance between the contents but each implies that the process is nearer to completion than observation might confirm.
78 S. S. Soeroto, *op. cit.*, pp. 289, 355.

translation was published. A Sundanese translation was published in 1930, a Javanese one in 1938 and, in that same year, a new Indonesian translation which by now has reached its sixth edition. There is also a Japanese translation (1955) and a French translation (1960). The Norton reissue of the English translation appeared in 1964 and in 1976, when the original Dutch version, with a new introduction, entered its fifth edition 'the English translation was republished by Oxford in Asia.[79] The first Kartini School was established in Indonesia in 1913, although one might question whether Kartini would have recognised in these schools the 'dream of their girlhood'.[80]

Jean Taylor, in her article 'Raden Ajeng Kartini' has shown how Abendanon, by his selection of the letters, has to some extent formed the historical Kartini.[81] We know her as she revealed herself to ten of her Dutch friends, as they revealed her letters to Abendanon and as he revealed them to the public. Stella, for example, burnt about 20 to 25 of her letters rather than hand them over. Annie Glaser was not prepared to have anything to do with anyone who asked her about Kartini.[82] Many of the letters to the Abendanons, which make up half the collection, are limited to extracts only.[83]

The English translation by Agnes Louise Symmers is a selection from the Dutch which includes only 78 of the original 106 letters. The Indonesian translation is also a selection and, in the later translation, it has been further reduced in the interests of economy—a smaller, cheaper and therefore more accessible edition but also more restricted in content.

I want to look more closely at the English edition, first published in the Norton Library in 1964 but, as far as the text is concerned, an unrevised reprint of the 1920 translation. This is probably the most readily available edition in Melbourne. It has an introduction by Hildred Geertz, is classified as Sociology and is one of the volumes sponsored by the Asian Literature Programs of the Asia Society, part of the UNESCO Collection of Representative Works, Indonesian Series. Eleanor Roosevelt, in a brief Preface says:

> If we are to become cognizant of the oneness o humanity, regardless of race or creed or colour, this book will be one of the ways that we will learn.[84]

I agree with her, yet at the same time I wish to argue that Kartini greater than any of the moulds and frameworks within which different people have chosen to confine her.

---

79 *Archipel 13,* Salmon, Claudine, 'Essai di Bibliographie sur la Question Feminine en Indonesi', pp. 29-30.
80 *Letters,* p. 81. See also Abdoerachman, Mrs *S. K.,* 'My Recollections of the Kartini School in Jakarta' (typescript, April 1969. Phot copy in my possession); and S. S. Soeroto, *op. cit.,* pp. 406-11 where she argues that the Van Deventer Schools were closer to Kartini's own ideals than those established by the Kartini Foundation in her name. Kartini wanted a secondary boarding school educating girls for financial independence, not a primary school training them for housewifery.
81 Taylor, Jean, 'Raden Ajeng Kartini', *Signs, Journal of Women Culture and Society,* Vol. 1, No. 3, Part 1, Spring 1976, esp. p. 640 although the whole article raises issues with which I have not dealt adequately here. My thanks to Betty Feith for drawing this article to my attention.
82 S. S. Soeroto, *op. cit.,* p. 399, quoting Bouman, *Meer Lict Over Kartini.*
83 At the end he even has a series of isolated 'thoughts' from unpublished letters *(Door Duisternis tot Licht, DDTL,* pp. 386-7.) This style has been followed also at Rembang where sentences are embossed on the wall of the room in which Kartini died.
84 *Op. cit.,* p.5.

I do not know anything about the translator of the letters, Agnes Louise Symmers, apart from what can be learned from the introduction to the translation.[85] (This has been reprinted in the 1976 Oxford in Asia Paperback). She sees the chief interest of the letters as 'their value as a human document'. The letters 'breathe the mode spirit in all of its restless intensity', although they were written by 'a girl of the Orient, reared in an ancient and outworn civilization'. Symmers, appears to know very little about 'slumbering Java' and claim that 'the Regent of Japara... sent his daughters to the free grammar school for Europeans at Semarang so that they might learn Dutch', which was exactly what he refused to do. She observes perceptively that Kartini and her sisters were 'free very much as a delicately nurtured Victorian young lady would have been free, half a century ago'.[86] Cora Vreede-de Stuers makes a similar point when she comments that, had Kartini not been restricted by having Dutch as her primary Western language, she might have felt 'closer to the aristocratic women of England or Russia than to the brave bourgeois Dutchwoman Hilda van Suylenberg'.[87] Symmers does not seem fully aware of the agonising struggle which Kartini underwent because of the conflict between her own ambitions and her father's wishes. This too must have been paralleled in many mid-Victorian homes.

The translator sees it as a 'human interest' love story. Kartini 'fell in love like any Western girl' and would have lived happily ever after but for her untimely death. She says of Kartini'. Her interests were human, and not merely feministic—which cannot be said of our own feminism' and, having shown her colours in that matter, she then tends to play down Kartini's interest in her 'pale sisters who are struggling forward in the distant West'.[88]

At the outset, though, I must acknowledge my gratitude to her for the fact that she did translate these letters, making them more readily accessible to me than the original Dutch will ever be. Nevertheless, I would be very glad to see them re-translated accurately and more completely for I suspect that, in the process of translation and selection, Kartini's writings have, to some extent, been trivialised. Where the letters have been cut the selection has served to lessen the intellectual content and to decrease the interest in feminist issues.[89] There are obvious errors in translation, such as the one already mentioned, where ELS becomes a 'grammar school' instead of a primary school, or where 'vijf' is translated as 'six'. Letters are sometimes wrongly attributed. Most annoying of all, there is no indication in the text when sections or odd sentences have been omitted.[90] The translation has not been undertaken as a scholarly exercise, but as a romantic tale and this, I believe, does less than justice to Kartini.

---

85 This has a sickly sweet foreword by Louis Couperus and a more satisfying Introduction by Professor Sartono Kartodir at her historical and prophetic significance.
86 *Ibid.*, pp. xiii, xv. The 'modern spirit' to which she refers is the period immediately after World War I.
87 *Archipel 13*, p. 114. Because of similar limitations on my part I must thank Cathy Lowy for translating the article and making this point available to me. Charles Coppel has pointed out that the (cont.) illustration which appears there (opp. p. 12) shows a French lesson in progress. She did mention her study of French and her desire to study German, but English was on her programme after she had mastered German and Russian, as far as I know, was not so that the point would still hold. Letters, p. 90.
88 *Letters*, P. xvi, xiii, 31.
89 *Ibid.*, pp. 35, 36, 63.
90 'vijf' (DDTL, p. cf. *Letters*, p. 32). Kartini may have meant to say that she had five brothers and five sisters. Letter 8 has been attributed to Mrs Abendanon instead of to Mrs Ovink-Soer (*Letters*, p. 80 cf. DDTL, pp. 67-70) and letter 30 is to Stella and not to Mrs Abendanon (*Letters*, pp. 141-3, cf. DDTL, pp.173 ff). The reference to Roekmini (p. 142), 'You would like her if you could meet her' supports this

This effect is heightened by the title of the book, *Letters of a Javanese Princess*, and this suggests a degree of both insensitivity and snobbery on the part of the translator. Kartini, in her second letter to Stella, says:

> Am I a princess? No more than you yourself are one. The last prince of our house, from whom I am directly descended in the male line was, I believe, twenty-five generations back, but Mama [her stepmother] is closely related to the princely house of Madura .... But we do not give a two-pence for all that ... I remember how embarrassed we were last year, when the ladies of the Exposition for Woman's Work (18981 called us 'Princesses of Java' I despair of its ever being different. I do not know how many times I have said that we were not 'ferules' and still less princesses but they have grown accustomed to the glamour.[91]

At the other extreme from this, as far as interpretations go, we have Pramud a Ananda Toer's book *Pan il Aku Kartini Saja* ('Call me simply Kartini') a title taken from Kartini's first letter to Stella. Pramudya emphasises her opposition to indigenous feudalism and to Dutch colonial oppression. Again in her first letter she wrote, 'All our institutions are directly opposed to the progress for which I so long for the sake of our people'.[92] To strengthen his argument *Pramild* claims that Kartini and Kartono, the brother to whom Kartini felt so close and whom she hoped to join in the Netherlands, were children of a peasant mother, concubine of Sosroningrat. The family tree which Pramudya concocted[93] caused great offence to the family. It was one of the first things Ibu Kardinah mentioned to us when we met her in 1970. She wrote an article on this subject in *Bijdragen tot de Taal-, Land- en Volkenkunde van N.I.*[94]

To return to the English translation of the letters, I would like to look briefly at the introduction by Hildred Geertz, a sociological analysis which, at the first reading, I found so impressive. Now I less sure. Hildred Geertz is certainly familiar with Java and she sees Kartini's individual crisis of identity as both a response to a and a contribution to a similar crisis in Javanese cultural society.

> When the letters begin Kartini is twenty, still caught in the alternating optimism and despair of a thoughtful, rebellious adolescent. When the letters abruptly end with her death four years later, she has become a woman. She has discovered for

---

as Mrs Abendanon had met Roekmini. *Letters*, p. 35 has a whole page omitted or allegedly summarised in the penultimate paragraph 'We take deep interest in all that concerns the Women's Movement'. On p.36, Kartini's question as to whether Stella knows the author of *Hilda van Suylenberg* personally, is omitted. See also *Letters*, p. 36, cf. DDTL, p. 42.

91 *Letters*, pp. 37-8.
92 *Ibid.*, pp. 36, 31.
93 *Pramoedya Ananda Toer, Panggil Aku Kartini Sadja;* pada Kartini (Jakarta, Nusantara, 1962, 2 vols.), *Pramoedya Ananda Toer, Panggil Aku Kartini Sadja;* sebuah pengantar pada Kartini (Jakarta, Nusantara, 1962, 2 vols.), p. 37.
94 Entitled 'Kartini: De Feiten' [Kartini: The Facts] it is to be found in *Bijdragen TLV van NI.*, No. 122, 1966, pp. 283-9 and supported an article in the previous issue by Cora Vreede de Stuers 'Kartini: Feiten en Ficties' [Kartini: Facts and Fiction], *Ibid.*, No. *121*, 1965. This article appeared sixty seven years after the one written by Kartini when she was 16. I doubt whether many learned journals could equal that record, articles by two sisters, one published when the author was 20, the other when the author was 83.

herself who she is, whom she loves, and for whom she must fight. She has made her choices.

For Hildred Geertz the interest of the letters lies in Kartini's own internal struggle and I would be inclined to agree with her, though I interpret the struggle differently. She seems to have accepted, at least tentatively, a version similar to that of Pramudya. She sees Kartini as giving up her dream of going to Holland 'with obvious relief' and she talks of Kartini's 'uneventful little life' being preserved for posterity by Abendanon's use of her letters in his campaign for education. Hildred Geertz concludes that:

> the letters provide—for modern Javanese, Indonesians non-Westerners and Westerners alike—a moving human account of one person's courageous search for herself, for a viable purposeful life.[95]

She seems to believe that Kartini found this in the end.

Pramudya, by his myth of her peasant blood, and Hildred Geertz by her emphasis on Kartini's personal struggle as a microcosm of the national one, both seem to mythologise and depersonalise Kartini herself This process has been taken even further in the shrine established at Rembang and at her grave, where thousands of Indonesians go each April. One cannot escape the fact, as Pramudya wished to do, that she was an aristocrat moving in the highest Javanese and Netherlands Indies circle and that she was well known in the Netherlands. It was, in its time, hardly an insignificant little life.

As we do not have access to any of the letters she wrote to her family, we know her only as she presents herself to her Western friends Most of them are much older; even Stella, her kindred spirit, was five years her senior. She moved freely in their intellectual world, she communicated fluently with them in their own language and she was ready, as she wrote to Stella, 'To tell you all that I know about my country and my people'.[96] It is easy to underestimate her role and her attachment to that Javanese world. We would need to see the contribution she mad to the *Art of Batik and Its History* by Rouffaer and Juynbool, the contribution to the Exhibition in 1898 to which reference has already been made,[97] her work in promoting the woodcarving of Japara and other local crafts, her position as entrepreneur for the craftsmen and as a designer of some of their motifs.[98] All this can easily be overlooked by the Western reader. Her mysticism,[99] her love of gamelan,[100] (Ginonjing in particular) tend to be downplayed.

---

95 *Letters* (Introduction), pp. 8; 21; 26.
96 *Ibid.*, p. 36.
97 Footnote 28.
98 *Letters*, pp. 147, 180, 189, 197.
99 *Ibid.*, letter qu. p. 18, p. 146. Ibu Kardinah spoke of the close bond between Kartini and her clairvoyant brother, Kartono (Interview) S. S. Soeroto reports without comment several stories of this nature. *Op. cit.*, pp. 374-81.
100 *Letters*, pp. 146 ; 50.

Wedding at Rembang

Source: Koninklijk Instituut voor Taal Land- en Volkenkunde

The three sisters - from left to right:
Kartini, Roekmini and Kardinah

Source: Koninklijk Instituut voor Taal- Land- en Volkenkunde

What has always puzzled me about Kartini's letters especially the last ten written from Rembang, has been her sudden 'falling in love.' It has puzzled me even more since studying the wedding photograph.[101] Ibu Kardinah said to us, as she had to Dr Boumant 'Kartini is dead. I will say no more. Let the dead rest'. It is for this reason, fortified by Siti Soemandari Soeroto's interpretation and Professor Haryati Subadio's speculation, that I believe Kartini's personal life to have been a tragedy, moving inexorably and inevitably toward the fate that she so much dreaded, a polygamous marriage which ended all her high hopes and dreams. Betrayed by the father she loved so dearly and, because she was so like him in character, had resisted for so long; used as a political pawn by Van Kol and Abendanon who neither of them fully understood her educational ideals and objectives; deserted in her hour of need by Stella, to whom she once wrote, 'I do not know what would become of my life, if, as God forbid, we should ever become separated'[102] and burdened by the pressures of her new life and new responsibilities in a town whose climate, both physical and social, did not suit her, so that she could not even continue her correspondence (in a sense even her pen was taken away from her), she seems to have given up hope and slipped away. She had believed she would die young. She had told Kleintje, 'You must carry on our work'. She had told the wife of the mantri at Rembang that she would be staying there only eleven months. Perhaps her final disappointment may have come when the child she had so longed for was not a daughter but a son.[103]

Her ultimate triumph came as the spirit of the age finally pushed open the door through which, when it was half opened, she had caught a glimpse of the proud, independent, happy, self-reliant modern girl she longed in vain to emulate.[104] By then Kartini the pioneer was dead. The only note of triumph in this was her own firm belief in the ultimate victory of her cause,

> The freedom of women is inevitable; it is coming, but we cannot hasten it. The course of destiny cannot be turned aside, but in the end the triumph has been foreordained. We shall not be living to see it, but what will that matter? We have helped to break the path that leads to it, and that is a glorious privilege.[105]

---

101 While not necessarily subscribing to Josephine Tey's line of argument in *Daughter of Time*, it is clear from the photograph that Kartini's husband is considerably older. The crouching servant in the background suggests, as does other evidence, that the court at Rembang was considerably more traditional than that of Japara.

102 *Letters*, p. 85. There are no letters extant to Stella after Kartini's letter of 25 April, 1903. She had delayed several months before writing. She said, 'Oh Stella, do not make the loss of this great illusion harder to us by your sorrow. It is hard enough as it is. You have always known that it was my dearest wish to go to your country and to gather wisdom there for my own people. Let us never speak of it again' (p. 221). Stella's reaction, in a letter to Mrs Van Kol (26 September, 1904, perhaps before news of Kartini's death could have reached the Netherlands), was so strong that she was 'hardly capable of writing about the affair'. (See Bouman, *op. cit.*, p. 59). She saw it as a betrayal of Kartini's own self. 'Anybody, like her, a member of 'those who have been called', cannot relinquish the direction of her life, to fill the desires of one person'. She wrote both to Kartini and to her father criticising the marriage. S. S. Soeroto, *op. cit.*, p. 349.

103 Interview with Ibu Kardinah; S. S. Soeroto, *op. cit.*, p. 379, records that Kartini said, 'If the child is a girl I shall have a long life, but if it is a boy, I shall die soon'. See also *Letters*, p. 242.

104 *Letters*, p. 31.

105 *Ibid.*, p. 226, written 1 August 1903, three months before her marriage.

Perhaps she summed up something of what I have been trying to suggest in a letter to Mrs Abendanon, written in October 1902,

Letters from a true daughter of the Orient, from a real Javanese girl, thoughts from such a half-wild creature, written by herself in a European language, how interesting! If in despair we cry aloud our miseries in the Dutch language, again it is so very interesting. And if—which may God forbid—some day we should die of our broken hearts—then it would all be so terribly 'interesting'.[106]

---

106 *Ibid.*, p. 204.

Women in a Yogyakarta *Kampung*

Kadar Lucas

Yogyakarta municipality is run officially by a city mayor. The structure of the administration is unique compared with other provinces in Indonesia. The city has several administrative divisions called *kecamatan*, and each kecamatan has several *kampung*. A kampung in Yogyayakarta is a non-governmental administrative unit consisting of many households or *keluarga*. Each kampung is divided up into a number of Neighbourhood Associations (RT's), each made up of about eight households. The kampung is run by a committee with a chairman, who is chosen by the Neighbourhood Associations. They are volunteers, and receive no government funds of any kind. A kampung is used only for the middle and lower class living areas. The upper class living area is called *kompleks*, for example, Kompleks Bulaksumur, Sekip, Kotabaru, although the official administrative structure is the same as the kampung. People sometimes use the expression 'kampungan' to characterise lower class attitudes.

Nyutran kampung is situated in the southeastern part of the city of Yogyakarta in Central Java. 'Nyutran' comes from the word 'Nyutro', the name of a guard in the army of the Sultan of Yogyakarta. Originally the land in this kampung was given by the Sultan to the guard, 'Nyutro', in return for services to the Sultan. Since I was born and have lived in Nyutran kampung, all the examples in this paper are from there.

It used to be a pleasant bicycle ride of about two and a half kilometres from the main Yogyakarta post office at the bottom of Jalan Malioboro, to the kampung. You pass by the residence of the Paku Alam, the second 'royal' house of Yogya, and the Indonesian headquarters of the Taman Siswa educational movement. The kampung itself consists of five narrow lanes, the so called *gang*, and has a very mixed population of about two thousand people. There are rich and poor, educated and illiterate, all mixed together. On the one hand, are the handful of well-to-do businessmen, running the batik, tea and shoe factories, a couple of university lecturers, public servants, and a member of the Indonesian National Parliament (MPR). Then there are pensioned government officials, soldiers, casual labourers and *becak* drivers at the bottom of the scale. Most children go to school, either to a government school or to the Taman Siswa. The kampung is still rather conservative toward outsiders, and only recently have two Chinese families moved in to live. Some families accept students as boarders; mostly Javanese, as people are still reluctant to have student boarders from outside Java.

The kampung lifestyle in Nyutran is halfway between the city and the village, a mixture of both urban and rural. Most people know the names of the neighbours and the size of their families, if not the names of their children. They still even greet one another in the street. At least they will nod to each other if they have not been introduced. People don't call around much just for a chat any more, but they still come to visit when neighbours have babies, and usually when they are sick. Other customs are still followed, although now not everybody participates. For example, people still prepare special food for relatives and neighbours thirty-five days after a baby is born, cook rice cakes with some sweets before the Muslim fast month of Ramadhan begins, and still make boiled rice cakes on the great Idul Fitri day at the end of the fast.

Since the original inhabitants of the kampung were quite involved with the palace, its influence is still felt in certain ways. Women who laugh loudly, look around as they walk along, or sit with their knees wide apart are still looked down upon. Why do some women still follow these customs, while others just ignore them? The older women, including all my aunts, still think the old ways are important. They say 'As a woman, you will be respected if you have good manners'. The second group say 'Men are not bothered by these traditions, so why should women be'? Which group is right?

Three rights were not recognised in Kartini's world. Women could not continue studying, could not choose their own husbands and could not work in public. Today most women in Nyutran kampung feel they have all three opportunities open to them, at least superficially. But the real question is, are kampung women satisfied with their lot, or do they still need other opportunities to lead a fulfilling life?

Kartini's idea was when the mother is educated, the children will be brought up better. Educated women will have educated children, and the nation will be educated. But does this mean that a better education provides or guarantees their future? Of course nowadays children have a better education than their mothers and their grandmothers of Kartini's generation (who were mostly illiterate, like my grandmother), but they do not always earn more money than the parents did. My family once had two servants, a mother and her daughter aged about twelve years old. It was surprising for me to find that the mother was literate but the daughter was not. It seems that Kartini's idea of educating the mother to educate the children is nowadays only applicable to those social classes who are well enough off to be able to send their children to school.

Now let us see the role of women in the family. In general the husband is working to make money and does nothing in the house. This is the wife's job. She manages the money and spends it with or without her husbands knowledge. The husband has very little say in running the house. However outside household matters, the husband is the decision-maker and the wife will support his decisions, for example, about whether to send the children to the Taman Siswa or to a government school.

In families with children, respect will be given to the father first, then the mother, then the first child, then the second and so on. Older children are always responsible for younger siblings, and the eldest, whether a boy or a girl is always responsible for the younger ones. If the family has no servants, the children share the housework. The boy cleans up the garden, fetches up water from the well and the girl does the cooking, washing the clothes and dishes and does the ironing. It seems that girls are expected to do all the housekeeping and boys have a limited role. For example, boys are not supposed to do anything in the kitchen.

Weddings and funerals always are the occasion for big rituals in the kampung. In a traditional Javanese wedding, the women perform a leading role in ceremonies like breaking the egg, and in preparing a special symbolic meal for the bride and groom. In other words, it is the women who choose the rituals, and help the bridal couple perform them. At the funeral women perform the washing and dressing of the body for burial. They also prepare the food and other offerings *(sesajian)* to ensure the effectiveness of the rituals. While men arrange the seating and the bamboo marque, women dominate all other activities during the various ceremonies.

These roles have continued for many years and people including Kartini would not think of changing them. Kartini's idea about women was not to change housekeeping roles, she did not think about 'Women's Lib.' as people do today. We often hear that the Indonesian women do not need 'Women's Lib.' as some western women do as it was not the aim of Kartini's plan.

What kind of role do women have outside their homes? As I mentioned earlier, the kampung is run by a voluntary committee, which does all the administrative work, such as registration of families, handing on government instructions, or witnessing land transactions. For these services the Committee charges a small fee. The Committee is supposed to know all about the people in the kampung. The kampung celebrates the various national days (the most important of which is 17 August, Independence Day) by putting on various attractions, which are arranged by the kampung Committee. As in weddings and other family rituals it is the women who provide the food. For many years it was the wives of the members of the kampung Committee who did all the work, although they had no representative on the Committee. It seems that Kartini's ideas on emancipation took longer to be accepted in Nyutran kampung than in other parts of the nation. While we have had women doctors, journalists, lawyers and university lecturers for a long time, Nyutran did not have a woman on the kampung Committee. So this was a big step for women to participate formally in kampung activities, in their own right. After having their own women's committee, the activities broadened, not just preparing food on national days but also organising children's games and women's competitions. Some women were very enthusiastic about the new activities which helped cheer them up. People were becoming aware that a woman could enjoy something outside her home and family, apart from her work as a wife and mother. But what was really needed was a regular activity which could be accepted by everyone, which meant it had to be non-political and non-religious. In this way the *arisan* was introduced into the kampung, as a way of getting women out of the house for a couple of hours once a week.

For most women in the kampung, the arisan activities are very suitable. They do not have to leave home for a long time, they can bring their very young children and their husbands do not mind because the meetings are attended only by women. For many, this is the only opportunity during the week of talking to their neighbours.

What is an arisan?

An arisan is really a way of saving money, by a series of regular payments (weekly or monthly) which are made into a fund. At each meeting a person is chosen by lottery to receive the money collected at that meeting. If twenty people join the arisan, and each member pays one hundred *rupiah* each week, the collection distributed each time the arisan meets will be two thousand rupiah. The winner rotates around the group. A person cannot win the collection again until the names of the other nineteen members of the arisan have been drawn although she contributes a hundred rupiah every week along with everyone else.

The weekly contribution is usually based on the income of the poorest members, so that everyone can afford to join it. The weekly lottery money is quite a help to buy things which usually cannot be afforded. There is always the problem of trying to strike a balance between keeping the contribution as low as possible (to allow as many people to join), while making the lottery winnings worthwhile for buying something special. The very poor in the kampung still find the seemingly small weekly contribution of one hundred rupiah hard to manage. Also, if you see people outside your own home in the kampung, you need decent clothes which the poor do not have.

Take one of our next door neighbours for example. The husband is a casual labourer, who earns or used to earn about three hundred rupiah per day working in a batik factory. The price of rice if Yogya then was one hundred and fifty rupiah per kilogram. How can the wife of this family manage to have any spare money at all, with seven children all under twelve years of age? If she can feed her children and make them full once a day she is lucky. Four of them are already school age, but only two get a chance to go to school, while two of the boys stay home and help their mother look after the younger ones. The children look small and stunted.

The other next door family is very quiet and shy. They hardly ever talk to their neighbours, never greet anyone on the street and never go out except for a very important reason. The children seldom play outside of the home with other children, and the wife will not join the arisan because she does not know what to talk about with the neighbours.

It is different again with the next family along the street, the neighbours of the very poor family I spoke of first. They are one of the richest families in the kampung, with a car, colour television, several motor bikes, a telephone, lots of beautiful clothes, and many servants. They eat rice as much as they like with chicken or other meat every day. The wife does not join the arisan, but for a different reason, For her, the lottery money is too small, it is not worthwhile spending a couple of hours each week, just to win two thousand rupiah every nineteen weeks. Doesn't she need someone to talk to outside of the family? She has more than twenty labourers working at the back of the house in their batik factory. She can talk to any of them, any time she likes. Besides she has her own women's group, which always meets in her house. I will mention this group again later.

So, who. joins the arisan then? The majority of the women in the kampung join it, not primarily because of the money, but because it a kind of social obligation. When there are kampung activities which are supposed to be for everyone, you feel obliged to join in, if you do not participate then you will be considered as a snob. Women who are in the work force have already got something fulfilling to do outside the home. As the money from the arisan collection is not considered attractive to them, they will only join from social pressure

Eventually for some, the arisan does not satisfy them. These are the more educated women, who might still want to do things with their neighbours, but not just chatting and collecting money. The activities of the kampung Women's Committee today are more satisfy for women with some secondary school background (SMP.SMA). Most are drop outs from this level, with a few 'from university, who cannot g a full time job. They are busy earning money as traders, money and food sellers, dressmakers and part time servants. They work from economic necessity of course.

They attend the monthly meetings of the Women's Committee at the kampung hall to learn about first aid for kampung families. (Yogyakarta Foster Parents Plan assisted this program in the beginning.) They have approximately 20 trained health cadres. Each family member can ask for medicine from the cadre without any charge. Also the Women's Committee levies a compulsory contribution from each family in the kampung. This program has been of great value in increasing awareness about health problems and providing help when it is needed.

Sometimes at these monthly meetings there are cooking and cosmetic (make-up) demonstrations. Another monthly meeting deals with the business of the credit scheme—*(simpan pinjam*—borrowing and lending) when women can get loans at a low interest rate. Also at these meetings women bring hand-made products and food to sell. Besides these activities, the Women's Committee also organizes dressmaking courses, charging low fees, to encourage women in the kampung to learn a useful skill. Women who are interested in traditional music *(gamelan)* can join the gamelan playing group—a woman's orchestra.

The Women's Committee also organizes a kampung pre-school. Here the Foster Parents' Plan has again provided assistance, but the kindergarten still needs better equipment and salaries for the two teachers. Every Sunday classes are conducted for the children in drawing, as a weekend activity.

Working for the kampung women means earning money, it does not mean personal fulfilment, recognition as an individual or job satisfaction. Why doesn't kampung society recognise these goals of Women's Liberation? It is because women are not themselves aware that there are other important reasons for working. This may be because very few have the opportunity either to become qualified, or to get any job experience before they are married. If they have not had the opportunity to work, they cannot be blamed for not missing it when they are married. Lack of employment opportunities means women did not have much chance to work before they are married (even if they are qualified), which makes it harder to get a job for the rest of their life.

What about those women who are qualified but who give up their jobs after they are married? To take one of my neighbours as an example girl was a primary school teacher before she married, she supported the husband through a university course until he graduated. Some years later after the husband had become 'established' in his career and had become a lecturer, the wife stopped working. The husband said this was to let the wife have a 'break' after years of working. The other more important reason is that the wife's status as a lecturer's wife is higher than as a primary school teacher. The husband with the higher status job will not want the kampung to think that he is unable to support his family. Because most women work to make money, the kampung will not feel sorry for her even though she has given up her career as a teacher and recognition from colleagues. Her 'job satisfaction' or fulfilment in another role outside the home is not considered important by her husband or by kampung society. A woman may want to continue her career after her marriage if the status of her work is the same or higher than that derived from her husband's position or if her husband's income does not cover the family budget.

In some kampung families, women are the main bread winners. Most they work as traders. Their husbands if they are working, do not earn as much as the wife, although few husbands are completely dependent on their wives financially. The husband usually does not work because he does not have any qualifications, whereas the wife, if she is a good trader in the market, can earn enough money to support the family. So the husband stays at home and looks after the fighting cocks, singing birds, and, sometimes the children as well. Fifty years ago, in lower class families, more women used to go to the market, and the husband earned very little money. Only a few families are in this situation nowadays. Women who believe that the husband should work and the wife should stay at home feel sorry for these women but the women themselves are quite happy. They go to the market and do not feel worried about the children because the husband is at home. These women are, of course, very independent financially.

In the kampung of Nyutran, besides the non-religious and non-political activities of the kampung Women's Committee, there are two other groups as well. One is a Moslem group. They have regular talks about their faith, which are always preceded by chanting the Kor'an *(pengajian)*. This group is naturally limited in both its aims and its membership. Being smaller and from the same religious backgrounds, the members are closely knit, quite different from the arisan. Nobody pays, and meetings are held at the house of the rich family mentioned earlier. The wife who would not join the kampung arisan, provides the snacks and drinks each meeting.

The other group is a Catholic one, called *sembahyangan* from the word *sembahyang*, meaning to pray. At the meetings the members pray together. They also make a regular contribution, and the meeting place is rotated amongst members' homes. Most women are members of the kampung arisan and one of the religious groups as well.

From what I have said earlier it can be seen for various reasons, still prefer not to be in the because working means simply earning money so they sense of fulfilment which comes from having a Job. realize their full potential outside the home they and new opportunity, as well as education.

Women in the Workforce[*]

Yulfita Raharjo

To my Mother, Rabia Djayakusuma

> 'My husband thinks that being a good mother is the most important career there is. I think it's even more important than a career'.
> (Friedan, 1962: 329)

The Labour Force and the Unemployed
According to the 1971 Indonesian census, there were 1.9 million people classified as educated. Of these 1.2 million, or 63% were further classified as economically active. Among the economically active 82% were males and only 18% were females, yet females had a higher unemployment rate than males, ie. 19% and 13% respectively.

The level of unemployment among Indonesian educated women is far above the level for total women. According to Turnham (1971:53) and Blaug (1974:10) the typical unemployed persons in developing countries are young and relatively educated urban dependents who are looking for white collar jobs. Turnham. (1971:50-51) compared unemployed rates of different educational levels in selected developing countries, namely Colombia (1967) and Malaysia (1965), both broken down by sex, and Argentina (1965), India (1960-1961) and Ceylon (1963). From these countries he found that the unemployed as a group tended to be better educated, especially those who are young and inexperienced. They prefer to remain unemployed and wait for white collar jobs rather than accept lower paying jobs with low status. The same is likely to hold true for Indonesia as well.

Unemployment by Age
There is a great difference between the unemployment rates for those aged 15-24 and 25 years old and above. The highest rate can be noted for those aged 15-19. This group needs special consideration because they had just left High School and therefore had no working experience. Due to the high unemployment among the young and the young age structure of educated women, the overall unemployment rate among educated women is higher than among women as a whole.

Employment and Inexperience
One cause of high unemployment among educated women is their lack of skills and experience. This is due among other things to the present school system, which has produced people to solve problems little related to present needs and graduated people with specializations where no manpower needs exist (Department of Education and Culture, 1973:23).

---

[*] For technical reasons this version has been taken from the author's thesis and the footnotes and references are presented in the form used there.

Moreover the same report also mentioned that:

> ... if the need is there, the prerequisite skills, knowledge and attitudes of the graduates are lacking, all with the same basic result, unemployment.
>
> The school system from primary through higher education, is seen as the culprit, for it has not provided relevant education of high quality to those who later become members of the labour force.

A study of social demands of education shows that the majority of high school students hoped to enter an institution of higher education, but only around 50% of those were successful. The study suggests that the low continuation rate is due to the entrance examinations, a barrier for many applicants, and the limited number of openings, which accounted for the great numbers of rejections (Department of Education and Culture, 1973:19). Another factor which accounts for the low continuation rate is the relatively expensive tuition and fees for higher education.

There is a strong tendency among educated persons to have high job aspirations. The study mentioned above reports that the kinds of jobs students desire and expect are professional ones. It shows, using illustrative data from Padang in West Sumatra, managerial/administrative positions were expected by 60% of respondents, followed by 18% professional/technical positions and 11% office work. The majority selected the public sector, security, good working conditions and high salaries as their job aspirations.

However, a recent study of the employment experience of school leavers in ICO regencies in Indonesia made by the same institution show that among the unemployed 15% had been offered jobs and refused them; the rate for girls (20%) was twice that for boys (11%) (Department of Education and Culture, 1978).

Unemployment and Dependency
Of educated unemployed women 47% were children and 28% the wive of the head of household. The importance of dependency becomes very clear since these two categories cover three quarters (75%) of those who were unemployed.

Among the unemployed children the majority were aged 15-19, while among the wives the highest rate was found among those aged 40-44. It is difficult to explain the reasons for these patterns, but most probably the high rate among the young and children is due to their not being urgent job seekers. Moreover they are also inexperienced since they have only recently left school.

Similarly the high rate among middle-aged wives is also due to their not being urgent job seekers. Because they are educated and h generally discontinued child bearing, they seek new horizons by joining the labour market. On the other hand, they have to compete with other job seekers and find it hard to acquire appropriate jobs.

Socio-demographic Characteristics of Educated Females in the Labour Force.
Age - The total average age specific participation rates are higher among educated women (40%) than among the total of all women (33 The high rate among educated women is probably a result of their involvement in the formal sectors, where the census records of employment would be accurate, whereas among the total of all women, the majority is engaged in agriculture which is the sector mainly affected by the inappropriate census definition of work, since those who had been employed during the last season were not included in calculating the participation rate.

The patterns show that for the educated women the curve is an inverted U, with young and old at the bottom. The low rates for young educated women are because most of them are still attending school. Consequently educated women enter the labour force at a later age than Indonesian women in general. The low rates among the older and educated women are most probably due to retirement. As already mentioned, educated women are mostly engaged in office work and thus they have to retire at the age of 55.

On the other hand, the curve of the labour force participation rates for the total of all women shows very little variation from the late teens up to the age of 65 and over. This is a typical pattern where the majority of women are engaged in the agricultural sector, since those who are engaged in agriculture continue to be so for almost all of their lives.

Apart from the young and old ages mentioned above, both the age specific labour force participation curves are rather similar. Both show the highest rates around the ages of 30-40, by the time most of them have already stopped child-bearing.

Urban-rural residence - The average level of activity rates as well as the age specific rates are higher among educated women in rural areas than in urban areas. It is difficult to explain this phenomenon since it is generally believed that there are more opportunities in urban areas for educated persons. The reason may be that most educated rural women are engaged in teaching. Teaching is regarded as a social status job in rural areas, while other 'proper' jobs for educated women are lacking.

Another possibility is that educated women. in urban areas are less likely to work because they are more home and family oriented, as typical urban middle class women are more concerned with their social status, but this does not necessarily mean that they cannot earn money. Even though they do not work formally in offices they may earn money by being self-employed. Unfortunately, in most cases these types of economic activities are excluded from the census definition of work. The opportunity for such activities in rural areas is more limited. As a result, those educated women who live in the rural areas have higher activity rates compared to those in urban areas. A more detailed investigation is needed to understand the activities of Indonesian urban women.

Marital Status - In comparing the activity rates of educated women and Indonesian women in general by marital status, the results show that both have the same pattern in which the highest rate is among the divorced. Both groups also show that the lowest crude rate is found among single women. However, among the educated, after standardization the single is the highest.

What is interesting is that the unstandardized participation crude rates of married women regardless of education, are higher than those of single women. It is suggested that the crude rate for single women is reduced because they are usually young and still attending school. However using age specific rates Indonesian single women from age group 20-24 have higher participation rates than the married women and divorced.

Fertility - The relationship between fertility and female labour force participation has been discussed widely. one position claims a negative relationship between female employment and fertility (Blake, 1965:41), especially in industrialised societies. Another position holds that the relationship between these two variables is not always negative (Goldstein, 1972; Stycos and Weller, 1967), especially as shown by the experience of many developing countries. About the relationship between these two variables, Ware (1977:413) raises the problem:

> ... even though census-type data can show that wives who work outside their home have fewer children than their housebound peers, ... they cannot show whether wives who have fewer children in order to work, or whether wives who have fewer children for other reasons nevertheless find it easier to remain in the work force.

Since this thesis is also based on census type data, it is not possible to know the motivation for joining the labour force among the educated women with children who are in paid employment positions.

It can be noted that the lowest activity rates are found among women with 2, 3 and 4 children, while the highest is among women with no children and those with 6 children and over. It is not difficult to explain why women with no children have the highest participation rate. Interestingly the same rate is shown for those with 6 children and over. For those educated women with 6 children and over, the household tasks can be shared with the older children and, because they have many children, their economic motivations to enter the labour force are strong.

If one only concentrates on those women who were still in their childbearing period, those aged 15-49 years, the difference in the participation rates between women with one or more children narrows. With each additional child the likelihood of women participating in the labour force declines, even though it is true that the rates are low among the young ages (20-24) regardless of how many children they have. If this is the case, the number of children still living may not be an important factor in determining whether a woman is likely or unlikely to join the labour force. On the other hand, it could be suggested that the ages of children as well as age risk of pregnancy are considered as more important factors, at least in tile Indonesian setting.

Migration - Those who did not migrate had higher participation rates by comparison with migrants. This finding is not surprising since mobility, which is related to employment, education etc. occurs less among women than men. Most women do not have independent mobility. Mobility for women, both geographic as well as social, is mostly dependent on their fathers or husbands, which affects their potential for employment or pursuing a career. Especially in the younger age groups, only a small proportion of women had ever migrated. From age group 30-34 the percentages of those who had ever migrated increases. Usually around age 35 they are already married. Therefore, most probably, they followed their husbands as wives and not in response to a demand for their own abilities. As a result their movements had little effect on their economic activities.

Socio-Cultural Characteristics of Educated Females in the Labour Force.
In discussing sociocultural factors which affect female participation in the labour force, two variables will be used as controls, ethnicity and religion. Province will be used as a proxy for ethnicity.

Ethnicity - The idea of using ethnicity as a control variable is based on recognition of the fact that in some ethnic groups women are more inclined to join the labour force than in others. Although comparison of 1961 and 1971 census data is affected by the different definitions of work, there are some consistencies concerning female participation in the labour force, and the pattern also holds true for different social groups and after standardization by age. For example, in both censuses, as well as between the groups of the total of all women and of educated women, Yogyakarta was always among the highest for female labour force participation and the lowest was Jakarta. Therefore, as Jones (1974:8) mentioned, 'these differences, then, would appear to be real ones, to be explained by cultural, economic and other factors'.

Since Indonesia consists of many ethnic groups which differ from each other, it is difficult to make any generalizations on a national scale. Yet the census data do not provide information on cultural factors which might help to explain the differences of female participation in the labour force. In order to have a proper understanding of these differences, a depth study is needed of each ethnic group, for each is unique, although these groups do share in common the influence of their cultural histories in shaping their present ethnicity and so affecting their current attitudes to female labour force participation. To illustrate this argument, the example of Java and Minahasa in North Sulawesi will be used because data is readily available for these groups.

There is a strong reason to think that the high rates of female participation among the Javanese, especially in Yogyakarta, and Central Java, are due to cultural factors. Some studies of the Javanese (Geertz, 1965; Papanek, 1974; Stoler, 1977) back up this view. Three of them observed that, traditionally, Javanese women are economically very active (including those who are classified as upper class women. I have observed that women dominate certain sections of the market such as selling and buying batiks, herbs and other products for women In Yogyakarta it is common to see high social status women sitting in the market attending their business, accompanied or assisted by their young and educated daughters. This is also confirmed by data on female occupations which show that among the Javanese in

Yogyakarta, Central and East Java, the highest percentage, apart from the professions of teaching and nursing, is involved in sales. Compared to some other ethnic groups, this involvement of educated women in trade is unusual.

In some other ethnic groups, such as among the Sundanese, the involvement of educated women in trade, especially in the market, considered to lower their status. A Sundanese expression which h negative connotation about women in the market is *awewe pasar*, which literally means 'market woman' but carries the connotation of the English expression 'tramp'. Sometimes this expression is also us about women who refuse to follow the accepted ideal pattern of being a good woman and housewife.

Clearly the Javanese attach a different value to working women from, the Sundanese. It is quite possible that the difference is due to historical precedents. The Javanese experienced the rule of the Sultanate and working for the Sultan resulted in high social status only and low pay, To cover the household economic needs the wives had to seek opportunities of earning additional income, through selling and buying batiks, jewellery etc. This type of activity has been passed on through the generations and has become part of the cultural system.

The Sundanese, on the other hand, had no long tradition of the sultanates. Instead the educated high-ranking people worked for the Dutch colonial government and were well paid. Their wives conformed to the pattern set by the Dutch officials, which of course precluded commercial activities by the women (Papanek *et al.*, 1974:17).

The above analysis suggests that the economic activities in which the Javanese and the Sundanese are currently engaged are greatly influenced by their past experience, and this also possibly holds true for other ethnic groups.

In North Sulawesi there is a big difference between the participation of the total of all females and of educated females in the labour force. The educated women in North Sulawesi have the highest female participation in the labour force and this still holds true after standardization by age. Jones (1976:39) mentions that historically the Dutch Government preferred to employ government officials from certain ethnic groups, especially the Minahasan. It is quite possible that this historical precedent affects the highest educated females in the labour force in this ethnic group. Apart from teaching and nursing, the Minahasan educated women had a high percentage engaged in clerical works, outnumbered only by Jakarta.

Jakarta is somewhat different. As the capital city from the Dutch colonial period until today, it is inhabited by people of many different ethnic origins. Most of the educated women are migrants. However, the low rate of female participation in the labour force among women in Jakarta requires further consideration, especially among the educated middle class women. I was involved in one study dealing with middle class women in Jakarta and we observed that the contributions of women to the household income are substantial. Numerous husbands of the respondents openly mentioned that their salaries were only enough for half of the month. They had no idea how their wives were able to manage the household expenditures. Later on, depth interviews indicated that actually most of their wives were earning money. Very often they were engaged in 'big business' such as being middle women in real estate transactions,

Jewellery, sales, etc. Some of them commercialised their domestic skills by making cookies, by catering, or by dress-making.

Interestingly, few of the respondents described their economic activities as work. Some women explained that, in order to avoid taxation, they were reluctant to acknowledge their economic activities officially as 'work', but most of them referred to these activities as just *sambilan*, temporary, and they did not wish to claim them as work. If this is the case, it will explain the low rate of reporting of sambilan jobs in the census, which used a seven day reference period as the definition of work.

Religion - Surprisingly there are great similarities between Moslems and Christians in level as well as in pattern of participation of educated females in the labour force even though the proportion of educated women among Moslems is lower than for Christians and it is generally believed that the participation of females in the labour force among the Moslems is low (Youssef, 1974). This may be because Indonesia differs from other Moslem countries in having no seclusion or purdah system and so some of the more restrictive Moslem attitudes to women have little influence there. Therefore in the Indonesian setting it seems that religion is not important in determining whether an educated woman joins the labour force or not.

The lowest rates are shown in the category 'others' which is composed of Buddhists and Hindus. The majority of Hindus are Balinese but among educated women the majority are Buddhist of Chinese origin. It is generally believed that Chinese women who live in a very strict patriarchal family (Freedman, 1957) are constrained from joining the labour force. So the low rate of female participation among the Chinese may be explained as a reflection of the attitudes towards women. The same evidence was also found among Chinese women in Singapore (Freedman, 1957) and Malaysia (Jones, 1965). Moreover, the Buddhist and Chinese as distinct from Chinese of other religions, are likely to be more traditional in their behaviour. Also most of the Chinese women assisting in the family **business** may not be officially recorded as working.

The Educated Women at Work
What kinds of occupations do educated women have? In what sectors of the economy and work status are educated women engaged? How does their pattern differ from that of women in general?

Composition and Sectoral Distribution
The majority of educated women were engaged in professional and clerical occupations. For the whole nation, the professional category comprised 53% of educated women in the labour force, while the clerical category accounted for 19%. If the category 'looking for work' is excluded then the proportions of these two groups of occupations increase to 58% and 21% respectively.

The data further show that in general the distribution of major occupations by provinces is rather similar. Except for Jakarta, the category of professionals is the largest group while the clerical occupations are the next largest. This concentration of educated women in professional occupations is probably a reflection of the job opportunities available. Included in this category of professionals are such occupations as teaching and nursing. Most of these jobs are made available by the government through the Department of Education and Culture, and Health. Until today, outside Jakarta, the major employer is the government. There were few private employers in the regions where women can find employment, since until recently industry had hardly developed outside urban Java.

The picture for Jakarta is the opposite from the pattern described above for regions. The professional group in Jakarta constituted only 30% of all educated females in the labour force, while a larger proportion (37%) consisted of those working as clerks. The reason for this pattern of occupational distribution may lie in the fact that Jakarta is a major capital city. In addition, industry is also highly concentrated in the capital. Hence employment opportunities for women are diversified. Besides teaching and nursing, there are equal and even greater opportunities for educated women in the capital to be employed in other types of occupations. Many women in Jakarta can find employment in private enterprise, in administrative capacities. These latter occupational categories compete with teaching and nursing in the Jakarta setting.

The major occupational categories mentioned above are mainly grouped in government, and public and social services, if the labour force is classified by industrial categories. Those whose occupation were categorised as professionals were primarily working in public and social service institutions, such as hospitals and educational institutions. On the other hand, the majority of those whose occupations were classified as clerical were concentrated in government institutions, such as local and central government offices.

As the majority of educated women in the labour force were employed by the government and public and social institutions, in terms of work status the greatest number (166,000 or 76%) were employee Only 2% were employers and 11% were involved in self-employment or family businesses as own account and unpaid family workers.

Career Choice - There are some interesting features in the work patterns of Indonesian educated women. It is obvious that because of their educational background educated women enter new occupations, most commonly professional and clerical occupations in service industries. A closer examination of the occupations indicates that even though educated women have entered the modern sector as professionals and employees.

Looking at female participation in five Southeast Asian countries, Manderson (1979) reached a similar conclusion:

> This distinction between women's work and men's work is equally as marked in the clerical occupations, where men are clerks and women typists. Further, women work to men, regardless of occupation. In the past, economic independence did allow women some exercise of power, but even so, according to the letter of the law (and lore) women did not enjoy high status, their role was ancillary. Likewise, female nurses work to male doctors, female school teachers work to male headmasters, female secretaries work to male bosses, female machinists work to male supervisors.

Similarly Myrdal and Klein (1966) compared women in the labour for in Great Britain, America, Sweden and France and found that the majority of women in these countries were engaged in 'feminine' occupations, as teaching, medical services and office workers. This is surprising since these countries have had a long history of women's emancipation movements. Myrdal and Klein (1966:77) commented:

> The effect of emancipation has been, it seems to replace amateurs by professionals in the 'feminine' occupations rather than men by women in the masculine spheres of work, though there is a fair sprinkling of women in most of the latter to day.

and then concluded:

> ... after several decades of emancipation and professed equality of education and opportunity the traditional division of labour between sexes still persists, even though in a revised version ....

What is the motivation for an individual to choose a career? This is difficult to analyses since vocational choice is a complex matter and many factors are involved. It is believed that vocational behaviour starts from early life. Vocational decisions are congruent with self concept and personal orientation (Holland, 1966). Both family and school environments have also been considered important determinants (Astin, 1969:34), while Myrdal and Klein (1966) mention opportunities and social customs to be significant factors in vocational choice. The aspects mentioned by Holland and Astin can actually be grouped together as social customs. Self concept and personal orientation are a product of Interactions between one individual and the social customs of the society concerned. Hence what appeared as self concept or personal orientation is actually a reflection of social customs.

Cultural norms affect work preference and also influence work patterns. If the norms have a strong influence upon an individual woman, it appears that work preferences reflect the societal ideals for women. The work preferences of Indonesian educated women are in line with what society expects of them. The occupations of teaching and nursing are closely related to women's traditional roles as wives and mothers. In addition, the attraction of teaching and nursing to women is also due to the opportunities for employment. The same pattern is also found in other Southeast Asian countries where teaching and nursing are dominantly female occupations (Manderson, 1979).

However, even though the work patterns of the Indonesian educated women show great similarities with some developed countries and Southeast Asian countries, yet some differences can still be observed, giving each country its unique pattern. Apart from teaching, the second and the third major categories differ from one nation to another. For instance, in France and Sweden, pharmacology and dentistry are referred to as feminine jobs. In the United States women are employed in finance, insurance and real estate, while in Great Britain they have hardly any impact at all in these spheres (Myrdal and Klein, 1966:78). Sanderson (1979) reports that in Southeast Asian countries, except Singapore which is predominantly Chinese, women enjoy high participation in commerce. This is also true among Indonesian women as a whole but the second and third major categories among the educated women are clerical jobs followed by nursing.

The Characteristics of Educated and the Total of all Females in the Labour Force
When comparing the characteristics of educated females and the total of all females, only some variables can be used, since the information for the total of all females is limited by the published census data. The three variables which have been used as controls are age, marital status and urban-rural residence.

Analysis of the age data revealed that the age structure of educated females is relatively young and, consequently, there is a high percentage of single women in this group. Also educated females stay longer in school compared with the total of all women and this may affect the pattern of their entry into the labour force. Another difference is that most of the educated women live in urban areas.

These differences, to some extent, make the level as well as the patterns of participation of educated women and the total of all females in the labour force different. Educated females show a higher participation rate than the total of all women. In addition, since they are educated and live in urban areas, educated females in the labour force tend to be employed in the formal sector. Among the total of all women who are in the labour force, the majority are engaged in the agriculture sector. It should be noted that the rates for women as a whole are low but this may not be an accurate indication of current female participation since, in calculating the participation rate, the published data does not include those who were employed during the last season (Jones, 1974). This would in particular, affect the data for women engaged in the agricultural sector where work has marked seasonal variations.

The Relationship Between Education and Female Participation in the Labour Force
A comparison between educated females and the total of all females in the labour force shows that as a group the educated females have a somewhat higher participation rate (40%) than the total of all females (33%). Although, as mentioned, the difference might have been reduced if the published data had included those who participated during last season. It is also suggested that the rates for both groups have been greatly affected by the census definition of 'work', which does not cover those who participate in marginal jobs. Hence the comparison of the rates is somewhat artificial. Further analysis suggests that there is a tendency among Indonesian women, especially those in marginal jobs, to make use of their domestic skills rather than their formal education.

If this is the case, this indicates that education *per se* is not a good indicator of the likelihood of Indonesian women participating in the labour force. This is not to say that education can never explain female participation but the limitation of the published data and the Indonesian social environment result in inconclusive evidence. Therefore cultural factors would seem to be more crucial in understanding female participation in the labour force in a society like Indonesia.

It is these sociocultural factors which explain why the majority of educated females does not participate in the officially defined labour force even though they may in fact be engaged in marginal employment using domestic skills, as this is more compatible with the cultural values than making use of their formal training. Therefore I have used a sociocultural approach in an attempt to understand the situation rather than using indicators which are not appropriate to Indonesian setting.

The Socio-Demographic and Socio-Cultural Factors in the Educated Females in the Labour Force

In analysing how socio-demographic and sociocultural factors contribute to an explanation of differences in the labour force participation among educated females, some controlling variables were used. The results do not always follow the common findings of Western scholars working in developed countries. According to the literature, we might expect urban educated women, non-Moslems, and those who have migration experience to have higher participation rates. In Indonesia the reverse was true.

An Interpretation of the Findings

My interpretation has been inspired by many discussions concerning women, and especially concerning the question of whether the condition of women has been improved or worsened by modernization. This is relevant to the topic of my thesis, since education is a key factor in modernization. The findings have shown that educated women are more likely to be housewives than to join the labour force.

There are two schools of thought concerning the effect of modernization on women. Schwarz (1972) describes them as 'Optimistic' and pessimistic'. As indicated from these labels the 'optimistic' view sees a widening horizon with the modernization of the role of women, while the 'pessimistic' view predicts the reverse. Both schools support their arguments strongly. The advocates of the 'pessimistic' thesis rely on anthropological data which can be used to show that women were not a subordinate group in traditional cultures. Thus, they argue, the current position of women has not improved and has in fact become worse with modernization. On the other hand, the 'optimistic' theorists emphasise the economic benefits by arguing that modernization gives wider occupational options.

I make no attempt to judge between these schools of thought, since each has some validity. yet these approaches can be misleading because they ignore the fact that each society is unique and therefore a specific approach is needed if a closer understanding of any particular society is to be achieved. It is essential to understand the position of women within their overall social system. The activities they choose and the strategies they use are conditioned by their social system in their attempt to maximize their own forces within that environment. At first glance, when only looking at the figures for educated women who are not economically active, Indonesia might seem to be a clear example of the 'Pessimistic' view that modernization has had an adverse effect on the status of women. A closer examination of the findings in their sociocultural context suggests that educated Indonesian women often consciously choose to be housewives because they genuinely enjoy this role and it is clearly compatible with the whole Indonesian social system. Consequently, I argue that models based on Western experiences must be used with caution or they may yield results which do not reflect the reality of the Indonesian setting.

A further conclusion is that in depth studies, even if small and scattered, are important in complementing the more superficial quantitative data from sources such as the census. The findings show that from the census subset of educated women these women in some ethnic groups have consistently higher rates of female participation in the labour force than in others, but these distinctions are hidden in the national rates of female participation. Therefore more detailed studies are needed if a clear understanding of the educated females in the labour force in Indonesia is to be achieved.

*****

References

Astin, H.S., *The Woman Doctorate in America: Origin, Career and Family*, Russell Sage Foundation, 1969.

Blaug, M., *Education and the Unemployment in Developing Countries*, ILO, Geneva, 1974: 10.

Blake, J., 'Demographic Science and Redirection of Population Policy' in *Journal of Chronic Diseases*, 18: 1181-1200, Pergamon Press, Inc., New York, 1965.

Department of Education and Culture. *Education, Manpower Development and Employment in Indonesia*. Jakarta, 1973.

Department of Education and Culture. *The Employment Experience of School Leavers*. An interim report on a longitudinal study of Primary, Lower and Upper secondary school graduates in Indonesia. Jakarta, 1978.

Freedman, M., 'Chinese Family and Marriage in Singapore' in *Colonial Research Studies*, No.20, London, 1957.

Friedan, B., *The Feminine Mystique*. Grandview, New York, 1962.

Geertz, H., *The Javanese Family: A Study of Kinship and Socialization*, The Free Press, New York, 1961.

Goldstein, S., 'The Influence of Labour Force Participation and Education on Fertility in Thailand', in *Population Studies*, Vol. 26, No. 3, 1972.

Holland, J.L., *The Psychology of Vocational Choice*, Blaisdell Publishing Company, Massachusetts, 1966.

Hull, V.J., *Fertility, Socio-economic Status and the Position of Women in a Javanese Village*. Ph.D. thesis, Australian National University, 1975.

Jones, G., 'Female Participation in the Labour Force in a Plural Economy: the Malayan example', in *Malayan Economic Review*, Vol. 10, No. 2, October, 19 5.

Jones, G., *What Do We Know About the Labour Force in Indonesia?* Lembaga Demograft FEUI, Jakarta, 1974.

Jones, G., 'Religion and Education in Indonesia', in *Indonesia*, Cornell Modern Indonesian Project, 1976.

Sanderson, L., 'Women and Work: Continuities of the Past and Present' in *Kabar Seberang*, No.5, January, 1

Myrdal, A. and Klein, V., *Women's Two Roles. Home and Work.* Routledge & Kegan Paul Lt., London,

Myrdal, G., *Asian Drama*, Vol. II, Harmondsworth, Penguin Books, 1968.

Papanek, H., Ihromi, T.O., Raharjo, Y., 'Changes in the Status of Women and their Significance in the Process of Social Change: Indonesia Case Study'. Paper presented to the sixth International Conference on Asian History, International Association of Historians of Asia (IAHA), Yogyakarta, August, 1974.

Stoler, A., 'Changing Mode of Production Class Structure and Female Autonomy in Rural Java' in *Signs*, Vol. 3 No. 1. 1977: 74-8

Stycos and Weller, 'Female Working Roles and Fertility', in *Demography*, Vol. 4, *No.* 1, Population Association of America, Washington, D.C., 1967.

Turnham, D., *The Employment Problem in Less Developed Countries. A review of Evidence.* Development Centre of the Organization of the Economy Co-operation and Development, Employment Series, No.1, OCDE, Paris, 1971.

Youssef, N. H., *Women and Work in Developing Societies*, Population Monograph Series No.15, University of California, Institute of International Studies, Berkeley, 1974.

Ware, H., 'Fertility and Work-force Participation: The Experience of Melbourne Wives' in *Population Studies*, Vol.30, No.3, 1977.

The Search for Women in Indonesian History

Christine Dobbin

In the closing years of the eighteenth century the first major woman novelist in the English language wrote her earliest novel of any importance. In *Northanger Abbey*, Jane Austin constructs a scene on the outskirts of the city of Bath, in which the heroine, the hero and the hero's sister, out for a walk, discuss their literary tastes. The heroine has a confession to make.

I can,

she says,

> read poetry and plays, and things of that sort and do not dislike travels. But history, real history, real solemn history, I cannot be interested in.

She then continues:

> I read it a little as a duty, but it tells me nothing that does not either vex or weary me. The quarrels of popes and kings, with wars and pestilences, in every page; the men all so good for nothing, and hardly any women at all.[1]

On the subject of the absence of women in works of history, Kartini, despite her many remarks on the unenviable position of women in Javanese society, has nothing to say; but, writing just one hundred years after Jane Austin, she too has to confess that, although she loves literature so much,

> I am still struggling with the groundwork history. Not that I do not like history; think it is interesting and instructive, but the manner in which it is set down in school-books has little charm for me.[2]

It has by now become a commonplace for writers on women in history to point out that, until very recently, history has been so defined as to exclude women from its purview: war, statecraft, diplomacy, administration, the constitution, commerce and business have seemed to what was until recently an exclusively masculine profession to be the stuff of history. Where the odd woman does intrude her person into this welter of male activities, it has been difficult to know what to make of her. I remember an experience of my own as a first-year undergraduate in the days when the study of the Tudors and Stuarts was part of the staple diet of budding historians. It was impossible in this context to ignore Queen Elizabeth I, and we were heartily recommended a book by an Oxford historian, T.M. Parker's *The English Reformation to 1558*. In it, I found to my surprise that the Elizabethan Church Settlement,

---

1   Jane Austin, *Northanxer Abbey* (Harmondsworth, 1972), p. 123.
2   R.A. Kartini, *Letters of a Javanese Princess* (New York, 1964), p.172.

that pillar of the modern Anglican Church, which I had naively supposed to be attributable to the English capacity for compromise and accommodation, was described as originating not only in Elizabeth's 'English taste for eclecticism' but also in her possession of 'a feminine disregard for complete consistency'.[3]

Leaving to one side such odd, towering figures of feminine inconsistency, in recent years much encouraging work has been done to redefine history and to produce what might be called 'people's history' history written not from the vantage point of those who have tried to run other people's lives, but from 'the real-life experience of people themselves'.[4] Here, of course, women and their life experiences loom much larger, and to certain branches of 'people's history'—such as, for example, the history of the family—they are central. Even in studies of the work-force, of the crowd, of popular religious movements and so on, despite problems of documentation, they can be seen to be coming into their own.

To me, however, a more encouraging development is the notion that we can retain history in all its variety—including wars, politics and diplomacy—if we simply accept Carl Degler's argument that, since women are not men socially just as they are not men physiologically, they affect history quite differently from the way men do, and history in turn affects them differently from the way it does men.[5] With this in mind, our perception of the past will be different too. Events which disrupt and restrict the lives of men, such as the two world wars of this century, may be seen to have opened up new opportunities and possibilities for women. On the other hand, social changes which improve the position of men can often be seen to have had a deleterious effect on women; examples are the organization of the early trade union movement, and the professionalization of certain jobs or callings, both of which led to the exclusion of women from certain areas of economic activity previously open to then. In any case, it should no longer be possible for the historian to write about a particular period or problem, discuss only the ways in which men's lives were shaped, and assume that therein women's lives are subsumed.

Tonight, therefore, I want largely to ignore both women as the subject of biography, and the redefinition of history to include social history, and instead concern myself with this last approach to women in history. If we want to search for women in Indonesian history, it seems to me that one possible starting point is to focus on some recent contributions to Indonesian history and to look at their authors' historiographical preconceptions. For purposes of comparison it seems wise to choose a particular historical theme, and here the Indonesian nationalist movement would seem to be a sensible choice. Historians of this movement deal with a period and events for which there is ample source material, drawn not only from government documents but also from an active press and from the evidence presented by the camera, by newsreels, by oral testimony and by autobiography. Moreover, it is a subject of interest to us as one widely taught to undergraduates in Australian universities and to which Australians have contributed their own historiographical skills. My intention, therefore, is to

---

3   T.M. Parker, *The English Reformation to 1558* (London, 1950), p. 174.
4   R. Samuel (ed.), *Village Life and Labour* (London and Boston, 1975), p.xiii. See pp. xvii-xviii for some interesting remarks on women.
5   C.N. Degler, *Is There a History of Women?* (Oxford, 1975), pp.8 *et seq*. I am greatly indebted to this stimulating inaugural lecture.

look at three major books on Indonesian nationalism written in English over a period of twenty-five years, a-id see how women fare in these works. I should say at the outset that I am afraid they fare very badly.

Beginning with the apogee of Indonesian nationalism, the Indonesian national revolution, we can do no better than to consult Benedict Anderson's *Java in a Time of Revolution: Occupation and Resistance, 1944-1946*. There can be little doubt that this book would be better entitled *The Javanese Male in a Time of Revolution*. Its major theme is the role of Javanese youth—the *pemuda*—in the Indonesian revolution, but throughout the book the collective noun 'youth' is used to apply only to male personages, and indeed the term 'youth' and the plural noun 'youths' are used interchangeably.[6] The author sees the core of the Javanese male's 'life-arc' as the experience of education in a *pesantren*, which he describes in wistful terms; the pesantren experience, he tells us, reinforced in the young male the values of simplicity, cooperativeness, solidarity and selfless sincerity. 'Simplicity', he goes on, 'was not only the natural product of a close community of unmarried males, without servants or womenfolk. It also expressed the inner sense of the pesantren—with withdrawal from the ties and hierarchies of Javanese society, and the search for a meaning to life deeper than that contained in social relationships'.[7] This theme of the solidarity of the unmarried male recurs again and again in the book. At one point, small boys are described as watching their elder brothers with fascination, 'inextricably tied to the network of informal relationships between youths in the larger society';[8] another, Bung Tomn's evening broadcasts produce an explosion of fraternity, shared experience and solidarity, as 'pedicab drivers, peddlers, clerks and schoolboys stopped to listen to him together'.[9]

We might say that the exclusion of younger sisters and schoolgirls from this evocative prose is a trifling matter. To my mind, however, it betrays a falseness inherent in the whole argument. The pesantren never was 'a closed community of unmarried males, without servants or womenfolk'. The very earliest systematic reports concerning Javanese pesantren, which date from 1831 and continue on into the 1930s, make it clear that girls and women of all ages attended pesantren, though in fewer numbers than did men and boys.[10] Moreover, they were taught by female *guru*, often, though not always, the wives of the pesantren kiyai, and, on occasions, by the kiyai himself. In 1881 it was reported of Banten and the Priangan that many young girls could read and write solely as a result of their time in the pesantren.[11] This female santri activity, it is clear, was not just confined to daily visiting by

---

6   B.R.O'G. Anderson, *Java in a Time of Revolution: Occupation and Resistance, 1944-1946* (Ithaca and London, 1972), pp. 18, 19, 20, 30, 33, 108.
7   Ibid., pp. 5-6. For a similar viewpoint, see C. Geertz, in 'The Javanese Kijaji: The Changing Role of a Cultural Broker', *Comparative Studies in Society and History*, ii (1959-60), pp. 234-9.
8   Anderson, Java, p. 30.
9   Ibid., pp. 185-6.
10 J.A. van der Chijs, 'Bijdragen tot de geschiedenis van het inlandsch onderwijs in Nederiandsch-Indie, aan officiele bronnen ontleend', *Tijdschrift voor Indische Taal-, Lande en Volkenkude* (hereafter TBG), xiv (1864), pp. 229-232.
11 Ibid., p. 232; G.F. Pijper, *Fragmenta Islamica. Studien over het Islamisme in Nederlandsch-Indie* (Leiden, 1934), pp. 19-20, 22-4.

neighbourhood girls. In some pesantren women had their own permanent quarters.[12] Anderson's 'closed community of unmarried males' looks rather odd beside an account given to Dr G.F. Pijper by a Banten official in the early 1930s:

> My informant... was required by his father to spend part of his vacation in a pasantren near Pandeglang so that his religious education should not be neglected as a result of his attending a school. Here he met, through a fortunate accident, the fourteen-year old girl who was later to become his wife, for the life of the pasantren, too, can be poetical. She, along with some other girls, was staying as a santri in the pasantren, which consisted of several pondok's. Naturally firm discipline was maintained... This was in 1915. In 1931 there were, in this same locality, also other pasantren's containing students of both sexes'.[13]

Although there is not time to labour this point, what I have just said about the pesantren applies equally to the Islamic religious brotherhoods in Java. Returning *haji* wishing to build up a following for an innovative type of devotion would often address themselves to women, and women and men would participate equally in devotional meetings. Women's devotion to such guru certainly parallels the male *kiyai-santri* relationship of which Anderson speaks.[14]

Stemming from this carefully masculine delineation of the pemuda, there are several other points which can be made about *Java in a Time of Revolution*. One is that, in common with all books on Indonesian nationalism, much emphasis is placed on the organizational politics of the national revolution, and on the intellectual debates and disputes which characterized the relations of the different organizations. The bewildering variety of organizations which are extensively dealt with are, however, all male-created and male-dominated bodies. For example, much is made of the Jaws Hokokai, inaugurated by the Japanese towards the end of the occupation, and of its associate the Barisan Pelopor, which, we are told,

> ... pushed the elite youth out into the masses and sucked uneducated youth up towards the elite .... To youths of all strata who encountered one another through the Barisan Pelopor, the experience generated that sense of mass power, of fraternal solidarity, of immense possibilities, that lies at the heart of popular nationalism.[15]

The women's affiliate of the Hokokai, the Fujinkai, it would seem, deserves no comment. In fact, for elite older women and for female pemuda, the Fujinkai served as heady a function as did the Barisan Pelopor; one which, one might even argue, was qualitatively deeper and more profound, as elite women were brought into contact with the mass of the urban poor, for whom

---

12 L.W.C. van den Berg, *De Mohammedaansche Geestelijkheid en de Geestelijke Goederen op Java en Madoera* (Batavia and The Hague, 1881), p.24.
13 Pijper, *Fragmenta Islamica*, pp. 22, 107.
14 Ibid., p. 23.
15 L.W.C. van den Berg, 'Over de devotie der Naqsjibendijah in de Indischen Archipel', TBG, xxviii (1883); pp. 162, 164, cf. Anderson, *Java*, p.6.

literacy classes, cooperative kitchens and a wide variety of other ameliorative schemes were provided.[16]

This is not merely an isolated example. Anderson's book consistently fails to deal with the female pemuda and with the general spectrum of women's organizational activity in the revolutionary period up to 1946. Only four women's organizations are mentioned in the text, and then solely by name, with no comment.[17] Except for one bald footnote,[18] none of the three major women's organizations of the period, Perwani, Perwari and Kowani, is mentioned. 'Merdeka' for the pemuda is seen as 'an experience of personal liberation',[19] which apparently constituted riding free on public transport, scrawling slogans on doors and walls, emptying bank tills, and, of course, killing Of the women's groups and congresses of the period, which helped to organize supply lines, liaison officers, nursing facilities and so on, and which must have provided a profound sense of 'merdeka' for the women involved, nothing is heard.[20] In fact, apart from a few isolated female names inserted into the text, with no indication of their owners' significance,[21] women as a category appear in a particular guise only: as the subjects of ownership disputes among soldiers;[22] with reference to Bung Tomo's vow of sexual abstinence;[23] and as a means of providing a sidelight on Tan Malaka's character because, allegedly, he refused to discuss them in a sexual content.[24]

Towards the end of *Java in a Time of Revolution* we come to a chapter on Social Revolution. Our author now confesses that an almost exclusive focus on national leaders and national movements 'scarcely does justice to the richness and density of the revolutionary process as it was experienced in Java in those days'.[25] Here, at last, we might expect to find some discussion of the impact of the revolution on women. Inde hope rises when we read that 'the common people came for a while into their own',[26] only to be dashed to find that social revolution is defined as the so-called 'social revolutions of late 1945 and early 1946, which were a sort of commoners' reaction to the persistence of bureaucratic and aristocratic privilege. Anderson is moved by the failure of these 'revolutions'; he ends his book with the paragraph:

---

16 Anderson, *Java*, p. 30.
17 C. Vreede-De Stuers, *The Indonesian Woman. Struggles* and Achievements, (The Hague, 1960), p.114.
18 Anderson, *Java*, pp. 93, 254, 256, 293, 437. The organizations are the Fujinkai, Persatuan Pemuda Puteri Indonesia, Perwani and Istri [*sic*] Indonesia.
19 Anderson, *Java*, p. 293, ftn, 53, where Perwani is mentioned.
20 *Ibid.*, p. 185.
21 Vreede-De Stuers, *Indonesian Woman*, pp. 114-6.
22 Of the 144 biographies given in the Biographical Appendix, only are those of women: Maria Ulfah Santoso, Setiati and S.K. Trimurti. These three also appear in the text. Maria Ulfah Santoso is mentioned on p. 320 as a minister in Sjahrir's cabinet; S.K. Trimurti appears on p.7 as a pemuda [*sic*] appointee to the committee to plan the establishment of the Gerakan Rakjat Baru, on pp. 92-3 as a pemuda member of PNI- Staatspartij and on pp. 260, 276, 314 and 446 in a number of the capacities; Setiati appears on p. 226 as a member of the working committee to organize the Serikat Rakjat Indonesia.
23 Anderson, *Java*, p. 34.
24 *Ibid.*, p. 157.
25 *Ibid.*, p. 276, ftn. 21.
26 *Ibid.*, p. 332.

Thus the revolution never became more than 'national revolution'; it ended in 1949, the Dutch transferred legal sovereignty over the archipelago into Indonesian hands .... Long after Indonesian sovereignty was recognized by the world, the search for 100 percent merdeka was to continue, and was to remain sentenced to disappointment. But the hopes are still with us.[27]

What of the hopes and expectations of Java's women in all this? What of their unending struggle in the field of family law, from the time of Kartini on? What of the very serious attempts made by the Republic in the Yogyakarta period to tackle issues of very great interest to women, and particularly issues affecting their position in the family? We might mention Act No. 22 of 1946 making compulsory the registration or marriages, repudiations and retractions of repudiations, or Instruction No. 4 of 1947 issued by the Minister of Religion which advised civil servants to try to dissuade husbands from repudiating their wives and to warn men of certain obligations in cases of polygamy.[28] Can we really say that, after the revolution, women's hopes 'remain sentenced to disappointment' in Indonesia?[29] For women across a wide social spectrum the term 'social revolution'—when compared with the stifling world of the Javanese female elite portrayed in Kartini's letters—has a very real significance, and to confine its meaning to certain maleinitiated political *coups*, with no concern for the wider social processes affecting men and women, their jobs and their lives, is truly a condemnation of history, political science and sociology as disciplines concerned with the condition and fate of humanity.

The second book I want to refer to relates to an earlier period of Indonesian nationalism, and is John Ingleson's *Road to Exile: The Indonesian Nationalist Movement 1927-1934*. Again the absence of women in the text is striking, even though the professed aim of the book is to 'contribute to a better understanding of the conflict of views, attitudes and programs in these years when many Indonesians struggled to work out what kind of independent Indonesia they wanted ...'.[30] Can we deny that the shape an independent Indonesia would take was of vital importance to the numerous women's organizations active in this period, as it was to female members of the so-called 'national' organizations? Moreover, the question of woman's place in the new Indonesia was discussed and reflected upon by many thoughtful men. If the founding of the PPPKI federation in 1927 was a triumph for 'secular nationalism', the achievement of which is carefully documented in Ingleson's book,[31] so too was the holding of the first Indonesian Women's Congress in Yogyakarta in December 1928, at which nearly thirty associations were represented and at which the federation of Indonesian women—the Perikatan Perempuan Indonesia—was established.[32] Neither the congress nor the federation is mentioned by Inglesen, although matters of vital concern to all members of the future

---

27 *Ibid.*
28 *Ibid.*, p. 409.
29 Vreede-De Stuers, *Indonesian Woman*, pp. 124.
30 See, for example, J.S. Katz and R.S. Katz, 'Legislating Social Change in a Developing Country: The New Indonesian Marriage Law Revisited', *The American Journal of Comparative Law*, xxvi (1978), 309-20. I am grateful to Hisako Nakamura for this reference, and her readiness to discuss this and similar issues with me.
31 J. Ingleson, Road to Exile: The Indonesian Nationalist Movement 1927-1934, (Singapore, 1979), p.vii.
32 *Ibid.*, pp.46-52.

Indonesian state were discussed, and although the Republic of Indonesia itself has honoured 22 December 1928, the day of the congress opening, with the title of Hari Ibu.

After his discussion of the PPPKI Ingleson charts the fate of various 'secular nationalist' organizations. There is no indication that women belonged to any of them, or that the women's movement influenced their programs in any way, although consideration of the 1928 PNI programme of action might have suggested some reflections along these lines;[33] consideration, too of Sukarno's popularity with the crowd might have allowed us to be shown some women's faces in the crowd, and indeed it is difficult to see how anyone writing after Rudé's works on the crowd in history can fail to notice them and ponder their significance.[34] We do meet them, of course, in their traditional role, on page 98 of Ingleson's work, selling red and white flowers *outside* PNI meetings.

Even if we ruthlessly exclude women from any business with these secular nationalist parties,[35] can we, in a consideration of the Indonesian nationalist movement between 1927 and 1934, ignore the new directions women took in this period? It was at this time that women's organizations became politicized. Splits and tensions over conflicting visions of the future became apparent. The 1930-31 split in the PNI ranks was parallelled by the splitting off from the women's movement in 1930 of the radical Isteri Sedar (The Alert Woman), which openly declared itself to be a political association and which put forward in 1932 a program not inferior in interest to that of, say, the PNI Baru.[36] Female secular nationalists and the women of the Islamic groupings contended with one another in this period in a context as intrinsically interesting as that of their male counterparts so carefully documented by Ingleson. Could we not, for example, have heard something about the split in the women's federation in 1932, which led to the establishment of Isteri Indonesia and the movement for the election of women to city and town councils?[37]

There seems little doubt, then, that Ingleson's work can be put into the same category as Anderson's. The male bias of the entire work is summed up in the author's treatment of the famous Youth Congress of October 1928 in Jakarta. Like Anderson, he sees 'youth' as a category applying only to males.[38] The 1928 Youth Congress he describes as 'one of the best remembered events in the history of the national movement as a whole....'.[39] Memory, however, is selective. The famous Sumpah Pemuda, the Oath of Youth, is translated:

---

33 Vreede-De Stuers, *Indonesian Woman*, pp. 89-90; 'Vrouwenbeweging (Inlandsche)', *Encyclope-adie van Nederlandsch-Indie* (Hereafter ENI), PP. vii (The Hague, 1935), pp. 971-2.

34 Ingleson, *Road to Exile*, p. 55. So, too, might the use of photographs. See J. Th.P. Blumberger, *De Nationalistische Beweging in Nederlandsch-Indie* (Haarlem, 1931), p.11-8, for an interesting photograph of a 1929 PNI meeting.

35 On Sukarno and his 'audience', see Ingleson, *Road to Exile*, pp. 98100, 159-61; cf. G. Rude', *The Crowd in History. A Study of Popular Disturbances in France and England 1730-1848* (New York, 1964), pp. 100, 105-6, 108-9, 114-6, 195.

36 See Ingleson, *Road to Exile*, p. vii for his definition of ' national' politics.

37 Vreede-De Stuers, *Indonesian Woman*, p. 93; Blumberger, *Nationalistische Beweging*, pp. 384-5.

38 Compare Ingleson, *Road to Exile*, pp. 127-32 with Vreede-De Stuers, *Indonesian Woman*, pp. 91-and Blumberger, *Nationalistische Beweging*, p. 385.

39 Ingleson, *Road to Exile*, p. 35, contains one passing reference to Putri Indonesia, the female branch of Jong Java.

1. We the youth of Indonesia have only one fatherland, Indonesia.
2. We have only one nation, the Indonesian nation.
3. We have only one language, the Indonesian language.[40]

In fact, each clause of the Oath begins 'Kami putera dan puteri Indonesia ...'.(We, the sons and daughters of Indonesia).[41] Indonesian female youth organizations were numerous in the decade before the 1928 Congress, and the recognition there accorded them represented the culmination of their strivings throughout this decade. Our author, however, continues:

> The solemnity of the recitation of the National Pledge, the raising of the red and white flag and the singing of the *Indonesia Raya* made a deep emotional impression on the youths present.[42]

The final work I wish to discuss tonight, if only briefly, is Robert Van Niel's *The Emergence of the Modern Indonesian Elite*, first published in 1960. This book covers roughly the period 1900 to 1927, and aims to explain 'the changes in leadership patterns in Indonesian society during the first quarter of the century'.[43] Van Niel explains that, in this period, 'the general course of Indonesian elite development was from a traditional, cosmologically oriented hereditary elite to a modern, welfare-state oriented, education-based elite'.[44] Here, one might expect, there would be ample room to ponder the meaning of the word 'traditional' and to discuss the part played by women in the emergence of this 'non-traditional' elite. We find, instead, only the compulsory nod in the direction of Kartini, and the bald phrase that girls' schools in this period 'produced Western educated young women who shared a changing social life with the educated Indonesian male elite'.[45]

Such a theme is capable of considerable elaboration. Even if we only look at Van Niel's elite in its organizational aspects, this is a period marked by a genuine blossoming of women's organizational life and associated journalistic endeavours.[46] One point may make my meaning clearer. Van Niel sympathetically depicts the role of the Dutch male ethici in stimulating the education and awareness of the Javanese in the early 1900s. Dutch women arriving in Java after 1900, however, are alleged to have in some way uniquely promoted ethnic exclusivity in the colony.[47] The notion that European men, before the coming of European women to the East, were able to foster racial harmony and comparability by taking local mistresses is, of course, a popular theme with male commentators on colonial race relations. In fact, as Kartini's letters show, the presence and concern of numbers of European women in Java's urban centres from about 1900 greatly encouraged and stimulated the Javanese female elite, and some of the earliest Javanese women's organizations were modelled on the Netherlands

---

40 *Ibid.*, p. 66.
41 *Ibid.*
42 See, for example, *45 Tahun Sumpah Pemuda* (Jakarta, 1974), p.69. This book contains some interesting photographs. I am grateful to Bill O'Malley for drawing it to my attention.
43 Ingleson, *Road to Exile*, p. 66.
44 R. Van Niel, *The Emergence of the Modern Indonesian Elite* (2nd impression, The Hague, 1910), p. 1.
45 *Ibid.*, pp. 1-2.
46 *Ibid.*, p. 35.
47 Blumberger, *Nationalistische Beweging*, p.160; *ENI*, p.vii, 970; Vreede-De Stuers, *Indonesian Woman*, pp.61-5.

Indies branch of the Nederlandsche Vrouwenbond ter Verhooging van het Zedelijk Bewustzijn (Dutch Women's Association for Elevation of the Moral Sense). Later, member of the Javanese female elite followed with interest the activities of the Indische Vereeniging voor Vrouwenkiesrecht (Indies Association for Women's Suffrage).[48] Urbanization in Java may have been for the male priyayi, as Van Niel suggests, the cause of much psychological difficulty, productive of the phenomenon of the marginal man',[49] but for many, previously marginal, elite women it offered new possibilities to meet, organize and agitate.

Without going into greater detail, the most important general point I want to make about Van Niel's book is that it is simply not enough to catalogue the activities of the members of the Budi Utomo, the Sarekat Islam and the PKI, to name but a few, and leave it at that. If the intellectual 'trends' among the early male graduates of western-style institutions of learning are interesting, so are those among comparable women. The views of the nine women consulted during the Declining Welfare Inquiry, published in 1914, make fascinating reading, concerned as they are not only with family matters but also with education, female wage rates, regulation of female labour etc.[50] The large numbers of women's organizations founded in the second decade of the twentieth century, too, deserve at least some mention; what, for example, of the Wanito Utomo of Yogyakarta, which encouraged lesser priyayi women to engage in commercial and business activities?[51] What 'of the significance of women in the earliest days of the Sarekat Islam, when so much of that organization's activities were directed towards fostering the batik trade? Tjokroaminoto's wife's business activities appear in a tantalising aside, yet we know that in the very highest levels of batik enterprises women took part in all major decisions, and were described by one observer as 'the soul of the business'.[52] What of the PKI's recognition of the importance of women in its propaganda

---

48 Van Niel, *Indonesian Elite*, pp. 8, 36-8.
49 *ENI*, pp. vii, 970; Blumberger, '*Nationalistische Beweging*, p. 151.
50 Van Niel, *Indonesian Elite*, p. 23.
51 *Onderzoek naar de Mindere Welvaart der Inlandsche bevolking op Java en Madoera*, pp. ix, b3: *Verheffing van de Inlandsche vrouw* (Batavia, 1914). For an English summary, see Vreede-De Stuers, *Indonesian Woman*, pp. 174-5.
52 M. Nakamura, 'The Crescent Arises Over the Banyan Tree: A Study of the Muha-dijah Movement in a Central Javanese Town' (Cornell University Ph.D. thesis 1976), pp. 94-5, ftn. 26.

machinery, and its very vigorous attempts to politicize them?[53] What of the very interesting 'women's mosque' movement in Java?[54]

The list is too long to continue. In conclusion, I should like to make it clear that the works I have chosen to discuss can be regarded as no more than a random sampling. I could have chosen other works in this field, by other authors, and come to similar conclusions. Nor must I neglect to note that my own works, both on India and Indonesia, have been influenced by the bias I have outlined tonight. The purpose of my talk has been to indicate that perhaps we can all do better next time. Surely a considerable period has elapsed since Kartini penned the lines: 'Everything for the man, and nothing for the woman, is our law and custom'.[55]

---

53 R.M.P. Soerachman, *Het Batikbedrijf in de Vorstenlanden* (Batavia, 1927), p. 39; cf. Van Niel, *Indonesian Elite*, p. 156.
54 *ENI*, pp. vii, 970-1.
55 Pijper, *Fragmenta Islamica*, pp. 1-58. 56. Kartini, *Letters*, p.42.

Right and Responsibility, Power and Privilege: Women's Roles in Contemporary Indonesia

Lenore Manderson

> Hardly a century has passed after Kartini has mid known her noble ideas and ideals about the emancipation of the Indonesian woman, and lo... the Indonesian Woman of Today has become the Equal of the Indonesian Man in every respect, in every field.[1]

Thus did the Indonesian Department of Information describe the status women in contemporary Indonesia: an especially optimistic view of the position of women in society and one not always held by the government.[2] Nevertheless, the formal recognition of the equality of women and men had been attained within the Provisional Constitution of the Republic of Indonesia in 1945 (Article 27), only forty years after Kartini's death. This constitutional acclamation of women's rights, and other legal measures introduced both prior to and after Independence, were rightly seen as significant advancements for women. However, these advancements have been enjoyed primarily by women of social and economic advantage, women who were the most restricts during Kartini's time.[3]

In this paper, I shall argue that despite legal and other formal gains for women made during the twentieth century, the status of women in Indonesian society generally has been little and less happily affect Upper class women have been able to take advantage of increased educational, employment, and political opportunities and have not been subj to social disapproval for doing so.[4] They have benefited from employment provisions and have gained some protection from the implementation of the marriage laws.[5] However, the majority of

---

1 Department of Information, Republic of Indonesia, *The Indonesian Women's Movement*, Jakarta: Department of Information, 1968: 5.

2 For example, the Indonesian country paper presented to the ASEAN Seminar of Women and Employment (Kuala Lumpur, 2-5 November 1976), prepared by officers of the Indonesian Department of Manpower, Transmigration and Co-operatives, assumed that equality within the workforce did not exist and considered ways of promoting equality of opportunity and treatment for women. The report noted that 'the pressure for action to improve their status in work life and society has been steadily rising everywhere'. Nana Soerya Atmadja and Simandjuntak BA, *Women and Employment in Indonesia*, a country paper prepared for the ASEAN Seminar on Women and Employment, Kuala Lumpur 2-5 November 1976, Jakarta: Department of Manpower, Transmigration and Co-operatives, November 1976: 1.

3 Cf. Cora Vreede-de Stuers, *The Indonesian Woman. Struggles and Achievements*, Gravenhage: Mouton and Co., 1960: 60. 'It was in the aristocratic circles of Java, where the lot of the woman left so much to be desired, that the efforts to break down barriers have proved more spectacular'.

4 Ann Ruth Willner, 'Expanding Women's Horizons in Indonesia: Toward Maximum Equality with Minimum Conflict', in B.B. Hering (ed.), *Indonesian Women: Some past and current Perspectives*, Brussels: Centre d'Etude du Sud Est Asiatique et d'Extreme Orient, 1976: 120. Also Atmadja and Simandjuntak, 1976: 12, note that; It seems that social attitudes and practices towards women in employment in Indonesia are rather favourable'.

5 Employment legislation is dealt with below. On the Indonesian marriage law, first presented in draft form in 1952 and finally enacted, after considerable dilution, in 1973 and implemented in 1975, see

Indonesian women, today in the past agricultural workers and petty traders, have been little affected by these changes and have both lost alternatives and power as a result of modernization and development. At the same time, they have been subject to attitudes expressed by public figures which increasingly stress the importance of women's traditional roles and responsibilities. A small and privileged group of women have had opened the doors of their 'prisons' but the reverse has occurred for peasant, working and middle class women in Indonesia.

*****

Kartini's rebellion against the status of *priyayi* women, women of noble birth of whom Kartini was one,[6] focussed as much on the attitudes towards women as on the effect of these attitudes on their lives'. In he letters, Kartini maintains that 'a girl is only a girl'[7] and that young boys were brought up to despise women and to regard them simply as a vehicle for their pleasure and convenience. 'How we women', she wrote, 'are degraded at every turn, again and again'.[8]

The daughters of the Javanese nobility enjoyed little freedom. From the late nineteenth century a few were sent to Dutch schools for an elementary education, but they were withdrawn to the confines of puberty whilst their brothers continued their education. Most girls, however, did not attend even elementary school; their formal education was limited to Koran reading classes which rarely provided them with bas functional literacy. Female education of course occurred informally. Young priyayi girls, like the daughters of the mass of Indonesians, were taught by their grandmothers, mothers, aunts, and older sisters to cook and to sew, to make *batik*, and sometimes to crochet, knit, and make tapestry: skills 'essential to make the girls good housewives'.[9] Thus the orientation of traditional female education within the priyayi class related directly to the vocational expectations of women. 'The only road which lies open to a Javanese girl, and above all to one of noble birth', Kartini wrote, 'is marriage ... it is a great misfortune for the woman to remain unmarried. It is a disgrace as well'.[10]

Kartini herself, horrified by the prospect of a marriage arrangement by her parents to a man of whom she had no prior acquaintance and of possibility of being only one of a permissible

---

especially Vreede-de Stuers, *The Indonesian Woman*, Chapters VI and VIII; her article, 'A propos du 'R.U.U.', Histoire d'une legislation matrimoniale', *Archipel* 8, 1974: 12-30; and Nani Soewondo, 'The Indonesian Marriage Law and its Implementation Regulation', *Archipel* 13, 1977: 284-93.

6   See Jean Stewart Taylor, 'Raden Adieng Kartini', *Signs, Journal of Women in Culture and Society*, Vol 1, No. 3, Spring 1976, 644-48, for details of Kartini's background and descent. Chr. L.M. Penders, 'Kartini: Indonesian Patriot and Reformer', in Hering, *Indonesian Women*, 21-3, discusses the declining role of the priyayi around the turn of the century.

7   Raden Adjeng Kartini, *Letters of a Javanese Princess*, Translated from the original Dutch by Agnes Louise Symmers, introduced by Hildred Geertz and with a Preface by Eleanor Roosevelt, New York: W.W. Norton, 1964 Ord ed.): 74.

8   *Letters of a Javanese Princess*, 140.

9   Hurustiati Subandrio, 'The respective roles of men and women in Indonesia', in Barbara E. Ward (ed.), *Women in the New Asia*, Paris: UNESCO, 1963: 232.

10 *Letters of a Javanese Princess*, 113-14, 154.

four wives or of being arbitrarily divorced, resisted marrying for some time. However, despite her 'deep aversion' to marriage, she recognized,

> ... some day or other it will come to pass, must come to pass, that I shall have to follow an unknown bridegroom... I can have no respect for the Javanese young man... he can torture (his wife) to death, mistreat her as he will; if he does not choose to give her back her freedom, then she can whistle to the moon for her rights.[11]

Kartini did succumb to the pressure placed on her by both her father and society at large. Her younger sisters, with whom she shared her ideals of greater freedom and rights for women, similarly were forced to concede to the demands of a society in which women had few roles to play and few options open to them.[12]

The life of a peasant girl at the turn of the century was no less prescribed but in fact considerably less circumscribed. Marriage and motherhood was also her prime vocation; she too had virtually no say in her marriage partner and was vulnerable to the same laws allowing polygamous unions and easy divorce. However, her days before marriage were less idly spent, for she was given responsibility early for the care of younger siblings and the preparation of family meals, and to assist with housework and to accompany her mother to the market place.[13] Marriage gave status to all girls, but it gave also to peasant girls considerable economic independence, autonomy, and power within the household and in village society at large.

Within the traditional peasant society, the Indonesian woman's role included that of wife and mother but embraced life beyond the marital home. Women established the nurseries and planted the rice seedlings; they harvested, dried, husked, and sold the grain. They tended vegetable gardens and fruit trees and cared for chickens, providing produce for sale and household use. In Bali, they were almost solely responsible for pig-breeding.[14] In accordance with both *adat* and Islam, they retained their rights to the property owned by them prior to marriage, and within marriage continued to own and dispose of property as single women. They were responsible for their debts and could take legal action. They dominated the market place, trading not only rice and other products of the soil, but also cloth, mats, and other handicrafts made in the home. Their role as traders continued despite changing economic circumstances in the twentieth century: as Geertz observed in the 1950s, 'the market is dominated by women, and even the rich successful wholesalers are as often women as men'.[15]

As a result of their participation at all levels of economic life, women enjoyed considerable power and influence within the household and the community. Tanner notes that in

---

11   *Ibid.*, 41-2.
12   One of her sisters had hoped to be a musician, but, realizing that it was 'absolutely impossible', resigned herself to the inevitable and chose to become a domestic science teacher instead. Even this was a radical choice for the day. *Letters of a Javanese Princess*, 126.
13   John F. Pembrook, 'The Role of Women in Traditional Bali', in Hering, *Indonesian Women*, 72-3.
14   *Ibid.*, 77.
15   Hildred Geertz, *The Javanese Family: A Study of Kinship and Socialization*, New York: The Free Press of Glencoe, 1961: 122.

Minangkabau society, ff mothers make most of the day-to-day decisions ... (including) land use, household management and expenditure, the education of children, lending and borrowing, and sale of handicrafts and agricultural produce'[16] and in Acehnese society, men are 'only minimally involved in family decision making; they do not control the purse strings, nor are they active participants in child rearing. These functions are centred on women'.[17] Similarly, Geertz maintains that 'the woman has more authority, influence and responsibility than her husband ... the persons of greatest influence are women'.[18] And, as Vreede-de Stuers argues in her classical work: 'It is the wife's importance as an active element in the rural economy that has determined her importance as a member of the community, where every action is guided by tradition and where everyone fulfils a function fixed with regard to the economy of the group'.[19]

The colonial administration generally worked within the framework of the traditional household economy. Stoler points out that women (an children) were neither excluded from the subsistence economy nor regard as replacements for male labour, but were a necessary additional labour force to men.[20] Women also participated in the plantation sector of the economy during the colonial period. A contemporary of Kartini, Dewi Sartika, who established a number of girls' schools in West Java in the early twentieth century, noted in her submission to the Dutch Government Inquiry into the Declining Welfare of the Native Population of Java and Madura (1914) that 'there is a considerable number of female labourers who have no professional training whatsoever and have at present to ear their bowl of rice in the factories and on plantations'.[21] In Bali, women were employed not only as agricultural labourers and plantation workers, but also as masons and roadworkers.[22] Thus women participated in domestic and national economic life and undertook low status tasks men were unwilling to perform.

While peasant women enjoyed influence and power within the community as a result of their economic role, noble women were ascribed political roles. In the absence of a male heir, a woman may ascend to the throne; they were in addition able to exercise political influence indirectly as consorts. Traditionally women were included in village councils and as religious

---

16 Nancy Tanner, 'Matrifocality in Indonesia and Africa and Among Black Americans', in Michelle Zimbalist Rosaldo and Louise Lamphere (eds.), *Woman, Culture and Society*, Stanford: Stanford University Press, 1-974, 144.
17 *Ibid.* 140.
18 Geertz, *The Javanese Family*, 78. See also Ann Stoler, 'Class Structure and Female Autonomy in Rural Java', in Kering, *Indonesian Women*, 137 (also published in slightly different form in *Signs*, 777, *Journal of Women in Culture and Society*, vol. 3, no. 1, 1, 74-89); and Robert R. Jay, *Javanese Villagers: Social Relations in Rural Modjokuto*, Cambridge, Mass.: The MIT Press, 1969, 92.
19 *The Indonesian Woman*, 43-4.
20 'Class Structure and Female Autonomy', 128. She argues that this had 'profound implications for the sexual allocation of labor'.
21 Cited in Vreede-de Stuers. *The Indonesian Woman*, 58.
22 Pembrook, 'The Role of Women in Traditional Bali', states that 'Balinese men do not particularly like working for wages, this they call 'coolie' work' (77). In not all parts of Indonesia was this the case: Willner, for example, notes a number of occupations from which women were excluded, 'Expanding Women's Horizons ...', 118.

and courtly functionaries.[23] These roles had established for twentieth century Indonesian women an assumed right and responsibility to participate in decision-making. It is therefore not at all extraordinary that women's associations were founded only shortly after the first men's voluntary organizations were established nor that women from 1912 were increasingly visible and outspoken in regional and later national political life.[24]

However, the women most capable and free to participate in twentieth century politics were for economic and educational reasons primarily women of the priyayi. Peasant women had neither the time nor the necessary skills to take part in the organizations established to challenge Dutch colonial rights and to establish a unique national identity for the islands of the archipelago. Neither were they therefore in a position to influence the direction which women's organizations took on behalf of all women. Thus, the women's organizations established from 1912, and those individual women pressing for change to the status of women, spoke primarily for their own group, that is, upper class women.

To 1930, their major concern was female education. Most women and women's organizations argued for increased educational opportunities for women within the context of the woman's role as wife and mother and especially as the first educator of her children. R.A. Siti Soendari, editor of the first women's journal, *Wanita Sworo*, contended that 'the Javanese people will not progress if Javanese women remain ignorant',[25] while Kartini, in her memorandum to the Dutch Government in 1903, stated:

> Can anyone deny that the woman has a great role to play in shaping society morally? She is precisely the person for it; she can contribute much, if not most, to raising society's moral standards. Nature itself has assigned this duty to women. As mothers, they are the first teachers of humankind; at their knee children first learn to feel, think and speak; and in most cases peoples' earliest upbringing influences their whole life. It is the mother who first plants in a person's heart the seeds of good and evil, which generally remains throughout one's whole life. It is not without reason that people say good and evil are imbibed with mother's milk. How can Javanese mothers train their children, then, if they themselves are uneducated? Never with the uplifting and development of the Javanese proceed vigorously so long as the woman is left behind with no role to play.[26]

---

23 See for example, Vreede-de Stuers, *The Indonesian Woman*, 44 ff. The reign of queens in Aceh is discussed at length in Iljas Sutan Pamenan, Rentjong Atjeh di tangan Wanita (Zaman Pemerintahan Radja Puteri di Atieh), Mimeograph, Jakarta: University of Jakarta, 1959.

24 On the establishment of women's organizations, see Denys Lombard, 'Apercu sur les associations feminines d'Indonesi', *Archipel* 13, 1977, 193208. Baroreh Baried discusses the Moslem women's association Aisyiyah, in 'Un mouvement de femmes musulmanes', *Archipel* 13, 1977, 129-35. See also Sujatin Kartowijono, 'Perkembangan Pergerakan Wanita Indonesia (Ceremah pada tanggal 21 Maret 1975 di Gedung Kebangkitan Nasional Jakarta), Jakarta: Yayasan Idayu, 1975; in English as 'The Awakening of the Women's Movement in Indonesia', in Hering, *Indonesian Women*, 3-19.

25 Vreede-de Stuers, *The Indonesian Woman*, 175.

26 'Educate the Javanese!' ('Geef den Javaan opvoeding!', a memorial addressed to the Dutch Government in January 1903), trans. and introduced by Jean Taylor, *Indonesia*, 17, April 1974, 86-7. An alternative translation of this memorandum is provided by Chr. L.M. Penders in 'Kartini: Indonesian Patriot and Reformer', in Hering, *Indonesian Women*, 20-48.

A few proponents of female education advocated a broader vocation education for girls. R. Dewi Sartika, for example, maintained that:

> it would be desirable... to train midwives, office-girls, typists, housekeepers, horticulturalists, etc, in short, all the professions which, according to conservative ideas, do not belong to women and have been up to now reserved for men.[27]

Generally however, advocates of female education believed the most appropriate subjects were 'feminine skills': skills which the students would have been taught informally in the home or which they would have learnt with marriage.

The first government vocational school for girls did not open until 1918, although private vocational schools had been operating from 1901.[28] Whilst in a statistical sense the number of girls attending schools increased dramatically during the early twentieth century—by 300 percent from 1908 to 1914—the proportion of girls in the whole society receiving any formal education other than Koran reading classes in fact remained minimal. According to the 1930 Census, only two percent of women (and ten percent of men) were literate, ie. could read and write in any language. Whilst the first Indonesian Women's Congress, meeting in December 1928 with representatives from 31 women's organizations, focussed on the establishment of schools for girls, the second general congress, held in 1935, drew attention to the continued problem of illiteracy. By the time, a number of women's organizations had established literacy classes as well as classes in the 'feminine arts'.[29] These continued after Independence had been attained.

By 1971, literacy rates amongst women had improved markedly. As Table 1 illustrates, some 46 percent of rural women and 70 percent of urban women were able to read and write; of women aged 10-14, 77 percent of rural dwellers and 89 of urban dwellers were literate.

Whilst the government was responsible for the improved literacy and education of younger women, women's organizations continued to play a major role in the eradication of illiteracy amongst adult women. KOWANI, the umbrella body of women's associations, for example organized an illiteracy eradication contest as part of its celebration of International Women's Year;[30] to play a greater role in the elimination of illiteracy amongst adult women.[31]

---

27 Vreede-de Stuers, *The Indonesian Woman*, 58.
28 *Ibid.*, 69-70.
29 Suiatin, in Hering, *Indonesian Women*, 14.
30 *Antara New Bulletin*, 14 October 1975.
31 *Ibid.*, 29 May 1975.

Table 1. Percentage distribution of literacy for population 10 years of age and over, by age, sex, and residence, Indonesia 1971.

	Urban		Rural	
Age	Men	Women	Men	Women
10-14	91.6	88.9	81.5	76.8
15-19	95.5	90.7	84.3	74.5
20-24	96.1	87.1	83.9	64.9
25-29	93.9	77.1	78.2	50.8
30-34	90.3	63.9	70.6	36.2
35-39	84.2	55.4	62.4	29.1
40-44	81.4	48.9	55.8	22.1
45-49	80.1	44.9	52.9	18.5
50-54	75.2	34.6	45.8	12.6
55-59	75.0	33.5	43.3	11.0
60-64	65.2	24.3	33.8	7.3
65-69	65.9	25.1	32.5	7.9
70-74	56.1	19.0	26.3	5.9
75+	49.2	17.9	23.0	5.6
TOTAL	88.3	70.0	68.5	46.1

Source: Republic of Indonesia, *Sensus Penduduk 1971*, Seri D, Jakarta: Biro Pusat Statistik, 1975, 61-66.

Despite increased educational opportunities for female education, steadily increasing enrolments and the increasing retention of girls at all levels of schooling,[32] the type of education made available to girls continued to relate to the perceived traditional roles of women. As Kartini and her contemporaries saw female education within the context of woman's prime vocation of wife and mother, so too women in the 1970s have been educated with this in mind. Women have been offered and have chosen subjects directly related to this role, such as domestic science subjects. At all levels of vocational education, women have been steered towards and have enrolled in firstly teacher training then health education courses. First educator of her children and guardian of her family's health, women seek training and subsequent employment as teachers and nurses within the larger community. Almost 56 percent of all graduates in health education in 1971 were female and over 40 percent of the education graduates were female. In contrast, a minimal number of women sought formal education in agriculture or commerce, even though the predominant traditional

---

32 The proportion of female students to total enrolments has noticeably improved even in recent years. For the years 1971-75, the percentage of female students at primary, junior and senior high schools was:

Level of Education	1971	1972	1973	1974	1975
Primary School	32	45	45	45	45
Junior High School	37	37	37	38	39
Senior High School	30	30	31	31	39
University	-	-	-	-	28

Source: Republic of Indonesia, *Indikator Sosial 1976*, Jakarta: Biro Pusat Statistik, 1977, 43-58.

occupations of Indonesian women have been in these two fields. As Table 2 illustrates, the proportion of women receiving training in areas neither related to women's social roles nor traditionally female is relatively low.[33]

Table 2. Percentage distribution of population 10 years of age and over by sex, vocational education attainment and field of education, Indonesia, 1971.

Level of Education	Sex	Agriculture	Technical	Communication	Health	Teaching	Other	Non-stated	Total
Junior High (Vocational)	M	2.1	40.9	0.6	1.9	33.8	12.4	8.4	100
	F	0.4	2.8	0.4	4.6	48.9	32.5	10.4	100
Senior High (Vocational)	M	3.5	25.6	1.1	2.0	43.9	17.4	6.2	100
	F	1.1	2.2	0.5	9.2	60.5	18.3	8.2	100
Academy	M	4.2	12.9	8.8	3.0	20.9	42.5	7.7	100
	F	2.5	3.8	3.3	8.4	35.2	37.0	9.7	100
University	M	3.3	11.8	1.2	8.5	30.4	37.3	7.4	100
	F	2.1	3.1	0.7	10.7	41.3	33.8	8.2	100
Total	M	2.9	30.7	1.5	2.5	36.2	18.7	7.5	100
	F	0.9	2.6	0.6	6.9	52.4	27.7	9.4	100
% Female		12.3	3.8	15.4	55.8	40.2	40.3	36.6	31.7

Source: Republic of Indonesia, *Sensus Penduduk 1971*, Seri D, Jakarta: Biro Pusat Statistik, 1975, 91-3.

Kartini saw education as a means of providing women with vocational choices beyond marriage and motherhood and as a means of attaining economic independence and freedom. However, some 70 years after her death, the majority of Indonesian women who had completed their schooling were primarily housewives and officially regarded as not economically active. Over 47 percent of all urban and 44 percent of all rural women aged 10 years and over were defined as housewives in the 1971 Census, whilst a total 33 percent (23 percent urban, 35 percent rural) were considered economically active.[34] A number of housewives would be women enjoying relatively high socioeconomic status, who had no economic need to work outside the house and whose husband could support the family alone. As Hull points out, 'being a housewife is a privilege, indicating that one is free to choose to stay at home'.[35] But the majority of housewives are not women in positions of financial advantage. Although the classification of economically active does include both employed and unemployed women, paid and unpaid workers, and women who may have several occupations of which only one is economically active, it tends to discount the economic

---

[33] However, educational attainment did not appear to be a criterion of occupational entry. Whilst some 57 percent of university and 47 percent of academy graduates were employed in professional, technical or related occupations, only 5 percent of women workers in these occupations were so qualified and 12 percent had no formal education at all. Similarly, 20 percent of women in administrative and managerial occupations had no formal education.

[34] Compared with the 1961 Census, when a total 23 percent of women were considered economically active.

[35] Valerie J. Hull, *Women in Java's Rural Middle Class: Progress or Regress?* Working Paper Series No. 3, Yogyakarta: Population Institute, Gadjah Mada University, 1976, 8. Hull notes a distressing tendency for middle class housewives to disapprove of working class women and to charge them with child neglect, 8-9.

nature of work undertaken by 'housewives': childbearing and rearing (one's own children, grandchildren, younger siblings and others), household cooking, cleaning, laundry, gardening, sewing, animal husbandry. The middle class housewives generally undertake fewer and fewer time-consuming tasks than poorer women[36] but all contribute to the household economy by their labour and production. Further, the majority of housewives, especially women in rural areas, do participate in economic life beyond the home; it is the sporadic nature of this work that results in its underenumeration. or discount in conventional national reckoning.

Advances in education have affected little the working lives of the majority of Indonesian women. Most have continued to do the same work as they did at the turn of the century: they were, in 1971, predominantly farmers or agricultural labourers; then petty traders and hawkers; then weavers, batik makers, and so on, producing handicrafts in their home alone or as piecework for small-scale industries. Many of these economically active women were divorced or widowed, but a considerable proportion were (and are) currently married and in some cases solely responsible for the household income.[37] Most had little or no education, as Table 3 illustrates.

---

36   *Ibid.*, 9.
37   Some 57 percent of divorced, 46 percent of widowed, and 34 percent of married women were considered economically active in 1971. According to the Census, 16 percent of all households at the time were headed by women. In 32 percent of urban and 28 percent of rural households headed by women, the women were under 40 years of age. A significant proportion were married.

Table 3: Economically active women by occupation and educational attainment, Indonesia, 1971, as (a) percentage of educational level, and (b) percentage of occupational category.

Educational Attainment		Occupation								
		Prof. & Technical	Admin. & Managerial	Clerical	Sales	Services	Farmers	Production, Transport	Others	Total
Nil	a)	0.4	0.0	0.2	13.8	5.2	63.0	8.3	9.1	100
	b)	11.9	19.9	13.2	61.5	62.6	65.2	54.5	48.7	60.1
Some elementary	a)	0.3	0.0	0.3	13.0	5.1	57.4	10.9	13.1	100
	b)	3.1	10.8	6.9	21.9	23.1	22.4	26.8	26.6	22.7
Elementary	a)	1.5	0.0	1.4	14.0	4.7	51.3	11.1	16.0	100
	b)	9.4	13.2	19.3	13.9	12.6	11.8	16.1	19.0	13.3
Junior High General	a)	16.8	0.6	4.3	15.9	3.9	17.1	10.0	21.3	100
	b)	11.3	10.4	21.3	1.7	1.1	0.4	1.5	2.7	1.4
Junior High Vocational	a)	56.7	0.9	8.1	7.4	1.2	8.8	5.4	11.5	100
	b)	22.0	8.2	6.9	0.4	0.2	0.1	0.5	0.8	0.8
Senior High General	a)	26.3	1.5	30.2	9.5	2.4	3.2	5.8	21.0	100
	b)	6.8	9.9	17.3	0.4	0.3	0.0	0.3	1.0	0.5
Senior High Vocational	a)	68.0	1.5	10.9	2.9	0.6	2.1	2.3	11.7	100
	b)	30.1	16.8	10.6	0.2	0.1	0.0	0.2	1.0	0.7
Academy	a)	46.7	3.6	22.8	2.6	1.8	0.9	2.8	18.8	100
	b)	2.2	4.3	2.4	0.0	0.0	0.0	0.0	0.2	0.1
University	a)	56.6	4.9	18.2	1.7	1.0	0.5	2.2	15.0	100
	b)	3.2	6.7	2.2	0.0	0.0	0.0	0.0	0.2	0.1
Total	a)	2.1	0.1	0.9	13.4	5.0	58.1	9.2	11.2	100
	b)	100	100	100	100	100	100	100	100	100

Source: Republik of Indonesia, *Sensus Penduduk, 1971*. Seri D. Jakarta: Biro Pusat Statistic, 1975, 206-8.

Women tended not only to concentrate in particular occupations and industries but also to comprise a significant proportion of the total workforce in those industries. Thus, for example, women were likely to be agricultural workers and agricultural workers were likely to be women. Conversely, occupations and industries attracting a few women were male dominated areas of the workforce. The proportion of women within industries, the 'feminisation' of industry, is presented in Table 4 together with the occupational status of women in industry. Industries with the highest proportion of women to the total workforce were, in 1971, agriculture, manufacturing, and trade and restaurants. Men participated in a wider range of occupations and industries in both traditional (mainly rural) and modern (mainly urban) sectors of the economy, taking advantage of new work opportunities created by industrialization and development. Women, on the other hand, have limited employment options and have tended to move from one area of traditional female employment to another. Stoler gives evidence of this in rural Java, where traditional home-pounding of rice (female labour) has been replaced by ricehullers (machines) and the traditional ani-ani for harvesting (intensive female and male labour).[38] As a result of these changes, poor women have been

---

38 Stoler, in Hering, *Indonesian Women*, 143-4; *Signs*, 87-8.

forced to seek alternate sources of income. They have largely ventured into small-scale trading to meet their subsistence requirements, gaining neither power nor wealth as a result of this economic activity. Further, by moving from agriculture to trade, women remain in a sector of the economy vulnerable to modernization and change and hence they may be further displaced.[39]

The predominance of working women in traditional sectors of the economy highlights their limited real opportunities and the small number of women in professions and in occupations not traditionally female indicate neither a changed role nor wider horizons for the mass of women.

The comparative occupational status of women and men provides further evidence of the essentially traditional nature of female employment. Proportionally and totally more men than women are own account workers and employers, then employees, then unpaid family workers. Conversely, women most often work as unpaid family workers, then as own account workers and employers, then as employees. The predominance of men as employees and own account workers and women as unpaid family workers indicates both women's work status within the community at large and the extent to which women rather than men have continued to work in traditional sectors of the economy. For example, own account workers and unpaid family workers in craft and production process occupations are likely to be making handicrafts in the home and be female; employees within the same occupational category are more likely to be working in factories and be male. Similarly, traditional sales workers include women hawkers, streets pedlars and stall holders; sales workers receiving wages or salaries for their work include shop assistants and salespersons and are predominantly male. Following the 1971 Census, only 24 percent of women in agriculture receive wages for their work; 52 percent are employed in unpaid capacities. Some 46 percent of women in the manufacturing industry and 10 percent of women in the trade and restaurant industry receive wages. Over 50 percent of all unpaid family workers in agriculture and community services, 60 percent in trade, and 73 percent in manufacturing were women: disproportionately high rates given the ratio of women to men in each industry (see Table 4).[40] The tendency for women to be employed without payment was most marked in those industries where women workers were concentrated; industries employing the least number of women workers and dominated by men, such as the transport, finance, and construction industries, had low proportions of unpaid female (and male) labour. However, within these industries women were also less likely to be own account workers or employers. Thus the concentration of women in traditional fields has allowed women some continued autonomy and independence.

---

39   Cf. Ester Boserup, *Woman's Role in Economic Development*, London: George Allen and Unwin Ltd., 1970, 95, notes that women traders are able to compete with modern types of trade and hence in rural areas the modern trade sector remains small. However, with the introduction of modern retail outlets, men not women are recruited as workers.

40   For comparative data of women own account workers and unpaid family workers to employees in Thailand, Malaysia, Singapore, and the Philippines, see Lenore Manderson, 'Women and Work: Continuities of the Past and Present', *Asia Teachers' Association Bulletin*, vol. 6, no. 2, June 1978, 11-13.

As a result of this concentration, the majority of women are not covered by employment provisions and protective legislation. Labour provisions introduced from 1948 include the Labour Act 12 of 1948 (jo. Act 1 of 1951), which prohibits women working at night, in the mines, or in work which may endanger her health or morality and which provides women with menstruation and maternity leave and special leave to breastfeed an infant. The provisions relating to night-work were still not operative twenty years after their enactment, and dispensation from earlier and more liberal provisions was granted. The prohibition against women working in moral or physical danger similarly was not enforced. Other provisions introduced subsequently have applied particularly to civil servants.[41] Thus a minority of women working in administrative and clerical positions in urban Indonesia, women usually of economic and educational advantage, have gained most from provisions relating to pensions, accidents, family allowances, and special leave. For the majority of women working outside the home, these regulations are either inappropriate or inapplicable.

Kartini and her successors constantly called on the colonial government and on Indonesian political leaders to grant to women the right and opportunity to participate fully in social and political life. But by the 1970s, this situation appeared to have reversed: government spokespersons and statesmen now called on women to take advantage of their right.

As development replaced independence as a major focus of Indonesia politics and government, so women were exhorted to participate in the process of modernization and industrialization. Leaders assumed that because woman had been granted formal equality with men, there were neither structural nor social barriers to their full participation. Sjaref Thajeb, Minister for Education and Culture, thus urged women to participate in development:

> Indonesian women must not only be housewives educating their children and providing their husbands with companionship, but must contribute through thought and deed to the development of the country and the glory of the nation ... Indonesia's independence gave to women opportunity for greater advancement. Because of this I call on women to increase their participation in modernization and development in *those fields appropriate to their nature and biology.*[42]

---

41   These include: -
- Act No. 80 of 1957, which ratifies ILO Convention 100 relating to equal remuneration for men and women undertaking work of equal value.
- Provisions of the Minister of Labour No. 3 of 1967, concerning financial assistance in respect of sickness, pregnancy, confinement, etc.
- Act No. 11 of 1969, which provides pensions for civil servants. There is no discrepancy in age of retirement for male and female workers. Additionally, a female civil servant who is the 'bread-winner' is entitled to the same family allowance as a male civil servant 'breadwinner'.

42   *Peranan Wanita Indonesia dalam Pembangunan*, Jakarta: Perkumpulan Pemberantasan Tuberkulosa, Panitya Harian Pameran Rumah Tangga, 1975, 39-41. My emphasis.

Table 4: Economically active women by industry and occupational status. Indonesia 1971, as a percentage of women by work status within industry, and b) percentage total workforce in each cell female.

Industry		Own Account Worker	Employer	Employee	Unpaid family worker	Seeking work for first time	Total
Agriculture, hunting	a)	20.9	3.0	23.5	51.7	-	100
	b)	17.3	24.1	32.2	50.3	-	18.5
Mining & quarrying	a)	6.7	6.6	74.5	12.2	-	100
	b)	10.4	17.6	6.0	22.5	-	7.1
Manufacturing	a)	29.2	1.6	45.5	23.9	-	100
	b)	48.5	14.7	34.7	72.5	-	42.6
Electricity, water & gas	a)	22.8	-	73.7	3.5	-	100
	b)	22.3	-	3.1	12.3	-	4.0
Construction	a)	7.7	3.1	82.7	6.5	-	100
	b)	1.5	1.4	1.8	4.7	-	1.8
Trade, restaurants	a)	.1	2.0	10.3	17.6	-	100
	b)	45.2	22.2	28.9	59.4	-	43.6
Transport	a)	13.1	5.4	77.2	4.4	-	100
	b)	1.0	2.4	1.8	3.0	-	1.6
Finance	a)	2.0	2.2	93.2	2.5	-	100
	b)	9.7	8.0	13.3	24.9	-	13.2
Community services, etc	a)	9.5	1.5	80.2	8.7	-	100
	b)	24.8	18.9	26.5	51.7	-	27.3
Not adequately described	a)	10.6	1.1	18.7	30.5	39.1	100
	b)	54.9	47.6	54.3	66.1	47.3	54.1
Total	a)	26.6	2.5	28.2	39.8	2.9	100
	b)	24.6	22.3	28.3	52.1	47.3	33.2

Source: Republic of Indonesia, *Sensus Penduduk 1971*, Seri D. Jakarta: Biro Pusat Statistik, 1975, 246.

As woman's role in development was to be guided if not determined by 'inherent' qualities, so too her failure to take full advantage of the opportunities available to her was related to her assumed nature rather than to prevalent social values and attitudes. Thus Ir Anwar Ibrahim, Head of the Bureau of Planning and Development (Biro Perencanaan dan Pembangunan) of the Department of Industry, maintained that:

> There are still many Indonesian women who are not playing a role in industry. They rarely have the ambition to reach high levels in the industrialization

process... women should take advantage of the opportunities available to participate in developments within industrialization.[43]

Whilst women were exhorted to participate in modernization and development, the traditional roles and duties of women were also stressed. Women were expected to contribute in life beyond the home but not at the expense of their home life. Woman's role of wife and mother remained her major responsibility and her prime contribution to the development effort. Mrs Tien Soeharto, wife of the president, told women journalists attending a training session that they should not neglect their duties at home nor the education of their children whilst carrying out their work responsibilities;[44] to wives of government officials she maintained:

> A harmonious and orderly household is a great contribution to the smooth running of development efforts ... it is the duty of the wife to see to it that her household is in order so that when her husband comes home from a busy day he will find peace and harmony at home. The children, too, will be happier and healthier...[45]

Similarly, the wife of the Minister for Religious Affairs exhorted wives of ministry officials to keep order and tranquillity in the home;[46] an article in the newspaper *Pelita*, entitled 'Women's Role in Development', described woman as 'queen' of the home and noted that whilst women were increasingly playing a role outside the home,

> ... women, especially mothers, must create a balance between activities in the home and activities outside the home.[47]

Statements such as these have largely been directed to middle class women, many of whom have chosen to be housewives. The interests of these women, as reflected by the activities of their organizations and the substance of women's columns in daily newspapers and women's journals, are nearer to the interests of Western middle class women than to the mass of Indonesian poor women: home and family, fashion and fortune.[48] However, these women often enjoy considerable status within the community and hence the attitudes which they hold towards woman's roles and duties tend to filter to other women.

Woman's prime role in development and modernization has been considered by many to be the fulfilment of her duty as wife and mother. Her immediate responsibility to her family is most often stressed, but she is responsible too for the future of the nation. Thus the Minister for Social Welfare has argued:

> Women cannot avoid their responsibility to use their rights for development and to play an active role in community affairs. On the other hand, we wish to avoid

---

43 *Kompas*, 6 March 1975.
44 *Antara News Bulletin*, 21 November 1975.
45 *Ibid.*, 26 November 1975.
46 *Ibid.*, 25 May 1975.
47 *Pelita*, 22 May 1975.
48 Hull appositely describes these women as belonging to a 'tingkat internasional', international class. See Valerie J. Hull, 'Fertility, Socio-economic Status, and the Position of Women in a Javanese Village', Ph.D. diss., A.N.U., 1975, 120-1.

any social disintegration as a result of development efforts ... the most vulnerable group in this respect is the younger generation, who it is hoped will carry these efforts into the future. Character and behaviour not guided as part of the socialization process will not accord with the norms and values of the society. The largest and most important part of the socialization process occurs within the family. And the one within the family who bears the responsibility and gives direction in this process is the housewife, ie. woman.[49]

As Hull illustrates, statements such as this would find considerable support amongst rural middle class housewives in Indonesia.[50] But women are not only the guardians of their children is morals and values, they are guardians also of culture and tradition. As such, women are given, if only rhetorically, enormous social responsibility:

We all have responsibilities which we must carry out. Some of these responsibilities women share with men. We now have women as well as men who are lawyers. We now have women doctors as well as men doctors. Together with m(n, we have women statisticians, scholars, politicians, and so on. We even have women prime ministers like Mrs Indira Gandhi in India and Mrs Bandaranaike in Sri Lanka. And, why not, we may yet have a woman president.

Clearly though, there are responsibilities of women which differ from those of men. These include those which have a biological basis, but many others have their roots in inherited cultural traditions and lores. These define the roles, rights and obligations of peoples of individual societies, including those which are believed to be the particular roles, rights, and obligations of women ... cultural traditions have much which is of value, fortune, and use, and for which we must fight and nurture, preserve and if possible develop.

Indeed, these cultural traditions serve to give us our identity as a nation, distinct from other nations.

Without our cultural traditions, we have no national identity; without our national identity, we have no nation.[51]

Thus woman's traditional roles of wife and mother have been stressed and extended within the context of national and economic development. Not inconsistently, her role in public life has been determined largely by her home roles. As illustrated above, women in the workforce working in non-traditional female areas of employment have found employment directly related to their wife-mother role—as nurses, as teachers, and as helpmates of men. Women work in the modern sector of the economy in support of and serving men: as typists, secretaries, and clerical assistants for example.

---

49 *Peranan Wanita Indonesia dalam Pembangunan*, 49.
50 Hull, *Women in Java's Rural Middle Class*, 8-9.
51 'Kaum Wanita dan Pembangunan Nasional di Asia Tenggara', speech delivered by Dr Sjarif Thajeb, Minister of Education and Culture of the Republic of Indonesia, at The Philippines Women's University, Manila, 25 January 1975, published in *Peranan Wanita Indonesia dalam Pembangunan*, 370.

In political as well as economic life, women have been relegated t support roles. Within political parties, they have joined the women's sections where they have dealt with matters of especial concern to women and the family while the men in the party proper have concerned themselves with the affairs of state. So-called women's issues have been supported by parties, but particularly at election time and jettisoned soon after. As Nani Suwondo notes:

> Usually before elections, political parties claim to support the demands for women's emancipation to attract women's votes, especially those who have not joined any party or women's section. But it has turned out that political issues are given precedence over women's interests, until the time before the next elections are drawing near and promises for the improvement of woman's position are renewed.[52]

Woman's main role within political parties has been again an extension of her private role: she is the supporter, the peace-maker, the stabilizing influence at time of crisis, the nurturer (of community based cadre), the sympathetic element in the event of distress.[53] In acquiescing to this image of woman as peace-maker and supporter, women have lost avenues of power and the exercise of influence; they themselves have sublimated women's needs to party pragmatism. The inability of the few women in public office and in parties to act cohesively on behalf o Indonesian women has compounded their inefficacy: it is not surprising therefore that the marriage act spent over twenty years in passage and was eventually implemented only after considerable dilution.[54]

*****

In considering the comparative roles of women in traditional and contemporary Indonesian society, it is clear that most women have attained equality only at a formal and theoretic level. Upper class women have made practical and recognisable gains, but it is this group whose lives were the most circumscribed in traditional society. The majority of Indonesian women have had neither the wealth nor opportunity to take advantage of formally introduced changes; meanwhile they have been vulnerable to broader social and economic changes over the decades.

Improved educational facilities and economic development have provided the daughters of the Indonesian upper class with the expertise and opportunity to move into non-traditional female areas of employment. In part, their participation in professional and administrative employment and their general involvement in decision-making was one of historical - accident: with independence, Indonesia had an immediate need for skilled personnel and depended on both women and men to meet this demand. However, traditional patterns of female participation in government and politics and the early 20th century political activities

---

52 Nani Suwondo, 'Indonesia', in International Institute for Differing Civilizations, *Women's Roles in the Development Tropical Countries*, Brussels: INCIDI, 1959, 342.
53 S.K. Trimurti, 'Peranan Wanita dalam Pergerakan Politik. Masa Lampau dan Masa Datang', Pustaka, no. 11, th.1, December 1977, 8.
54 Cf. Vreede-de Stuers, *The Indonesian Woman*, 138-40.

of a few women as well as men established a precedent for their involvement in modern public life.

But such opportunities were opportunities for the elite only. Both Wertheim and Vreede-de Stuers claim that, whilst women had fought side by side with men during the revolution, with peace and independence woman's role became clearly defined and confined: 'Women, no longer needed as partners in the struggle, began to see themselves ... relegated to the background'[55] ... 'women became competitors in the eyes of men to be feared even, since they were now capable of managing public as well as their own private affairs'.[56]

Of course, as earlier illustrated, Indonesian women have a tradition of managing public as well as private affairs and have continued to play an important role in economic life in post-independence Indonesia. It has certainly never been true for women in general that 'they have been taught for centuries to serve their husbands. Difficulties begin if the wife has carried out a task without her husband's knowledge *or without his approval.*'[57] But for the most part, they have undertaken jobs of low status and poor pay. Lower class Indonesian women have retained at least a measure of personal autonomy and economic independence, but of necessity not choice. Accordingly, as Hull argues, it would be false to assign a higher status vis-a-vis men to lower class working women than to middle class women who are economically dependent on their husbands.[58]

Rizali Noor suggests that modernization and development have had little effect on the lives of the majority of Indonesian women and on attitudes towards them held by both men and the women themselves:

> There is still a great discrepancy between equality in law and equality in practice in many of the developing countries where strong traditions, remnants of feudalism and illiteracy still prevail ... In a plural society like Indonesia where the influence of various religions, customary laws, traditions and taboos are still very much prevailing, especially in rural areas, the impact of modernization upon a country with such a cultural pattern can be seen only in the application of modern gadgets, electrical appliances, etc., but has yet brought little change to the basic behavioural attitudes of the population at large.[59]

However, what emerges from a consideration of published material and public statements of the 1970s is that attitudes towards women have been affected by modernization but not necessarily to women's advantage. For the majority of Indonesian women, illiterate peasants and labourers, there is neither a tradition of the confinement of women nor the prevalence of attitudes today which discourage their continued presence beyond the domestic sphere. The

---

55 W.F. Wertheim, *Indonesian Society in Transition: A Study of Social Change*, The Hague: W. van Hoeve, 1969 (1st pub. 1956), p. 142.
56 Vreede-de Stuers, *The Indonesian Woman*, 163.
57 Suiatin Kartowijono, 'The Awakening of the Women's Movement', p. 16. Her emphasis.
58 Hull, *Women in Java's Rural Middle Class*, 9-10.
59 Yetty Rizali Noor, 'Indonesian Women's Participation in Development', in Hering, *Indonesian Women*, pp. 159-60 (also published as 'Partisipasi Wanita Indonesia dalam Pembangunan', *Indonesia Magazine*, vol. 31, 1975, 5-14.

expression of attitudes of disapproval appear to be held primarily by educated women (and men of their class) whose privileged economic and social position grants to them a range of choices not entertained by the majority. These women are faced with a dilemma: they now have the right to participate fully in society and an especial responsibility to participate in development efforts, yet their major contribution to the nation is constantly seen in terms of their fulfilment of the traditional roles of wife and mother.

In the past, an upper class woman's life was spent in the expectation and the fulfilment of marriage and motherhood; she had neither power nor opportunity to choose otherwise. Today, her choice is open: for financial and educational reasons she is able to join other elite women and men in positions of power and prestige; she can afford domestic help to support her in doing so. For the middle class woman, the choice is less easily made: her lesser education and lower economic status relative to the upper class woman determines her employment in the workforce in a lower status, poorly paid, and stereotypical-female occupation.

She is vulnerable to attitudes questioning her right to act independently and autonomously; by choosing not to joining the workforce she gains prestige within her immediate community. For the lower class woman, there is no choice: the economics of her everyday life predetermine her participation in a limited number of traditional occupations in addition to her unquestioned responsibility to her home and family.

Notes on Contributors

Christine Dobbin, B.A. (Sydney), B.Phil.. D-Phil (Oxford), formerly lecturer in history at University of Lancaster, U.K. and at Flinders University, S.A. Her major publications are *Basic Documents in the Development of India and Pakistan, 1935-1947,* London, Van Nostrand Reinhold, 1970; Urban *Leadership in Western India: Politics and Communities in Bombay City, 1840-85,* Oxford, Oxford University Press, 1972; *Islamic Revivalism in a Changing Peasant Economy: Central Sumatra 1784-1847,* forthcoming 1981, Scandinavian Institute of Asian Studies Monograph Series. She is presently Visiting Fellow, Department of Pacific & South East Asian History, A.N.U.

Kadar Lucas, Drs (Gajah Mada), has worked in the Foster Parents' Plan Office and as Secretary of the Population Institute of Cajah Mada University. She is at present living in New Zealand where her husband, Anton, lectures at Auckland University.

Lenore Sanderson, B.A. (Asian Studies) and Ph.D. (A.N.U.), has published widely in the areas of demography, women in Southeast Asia and the anthropology of food and is author of *Women, Politics, and Change,* Kuala Lumpur, Oxford University Press, 1980. She is currently a post-doctoral research fellow with the Department of Indonesian and Malayan Studies, University of Sydney.

Yulfita Raharjo, Drs (Cajah Mada), M.A. (A.N.U.), is a Research Associate of Leknas, the National Economic and Cultural Research Institute. She presented her paper just prior to leaving for Indonesia to do research in the Blitar region of East Java on women's roles in Javanese village life.

Ailsa Thomson Zainu'ddin, B.A. Hons. (History and English), M.A., B.Ed. (Melbourne), Senior Lecturer, Education Faculty, Monash University, was a Volunteer Graduate for Indonesia and has written on various aspects of Indonesian history, education and culture. The second edition of her *Short History of Indonesia,* Cassell Australia, (1st edn. 1968) appeared earlier this year. Other publications include *Lagu-Lagu Indonesia/Songs of Indonesia,* Heinemann Education, 1969 and text books for Year 10 and (with Zainu'ddin) for Years 6-7. Her current research interests centre on the history of education for women. She has been a member of the Victorian Australian-Indonesian-Association since its foundation in 1956 and represents the Education Faculty on the Standing Committee of the Centre of Southeast Asian Studies.

The contribution made by Pam Sayers to the production of this volume has been invaluable as those concerned with the earlier volumes in this series will know very well.